The Role of the Mind
in
Discipleship

The Role of the Mind in Discipleship

Vikas A. Ram

ISPCK
Impacting Communities since 1710

2011

The Role of the Mind in Discipleship – published by Rev. Dr. Ashish Amos of Indian Society for Promoting Christian Knowledge (ISPCK), Post Box 1585, 1654, Madarsa Road, Kashmere Gate, Delhi-110006.

ISBN: 978-81-8465-142-3

Laser typeset by

ISPCK, Post Box 1585, 1654, Madarsa Road, Kashmere Gate, Delhi-110006 • *Tel:* 23866323

e-mail: ashish@ispck.org.in • ella@ispck.org.in
website: www.ispck.org.in

This book is dedicated to my parents,
Mr. Anoop and Mrs. Elizabeth Ram,
who were my real guides and mentors
during the formative years of my childhood.

"For with You is the fountain of life;

in Your light we see light"

Psalm 36:9

Contents

Acknowledgements

First and foremost, I thank God Almighty for his enabling grace!

I am thankful to my mentor, Dr. Cornelis Bennema, for his encouragement and support. His constructive criticisms and valuable insights have resulted in the present work.

I would also like to thank Rev. Dr. Ashish Amos, General Secretary, ISPCK, Mrs. Ella Sonawane, Mission Secretary, ISPCK, Mr. Rajesh Williams, Editor, ISPCK, and all the other members of the ISPCK team for their encouragement, support and cooperation in publishing this book.

Thanks are due to my friends, Col. Suresh and Nandita Ghorpade, Aardhana and Prateek Kashyap, Ashwani Jacob, Rev. Thomas Singh and Vijay C. Minz, who have acted like my think pads, providing me with feedbacks on my research work.

I would also like to thank senior leaders, such as Rev. Robert E. Clarke, Rev. Kuruvilla Chandy, Bro. Raju Mathew, Rev. Dr. Richard Howell, Pastor Prakash Masih and Rev. Prabhat Kashyap, for acting like mentors and spiritual guides in my life.

I am also grateful to servants of God, Dr. Ravi K. Zacharias, Dr. E. Stanley Jones, Bro. Rees Howell, Mr. D.P.Titus, Uncle Ron Fair for strengthening my faith and helping me make progress in my pilgrimage.

I would also like to express my gratitude to Dr. and Mrs. Graham Houghton for their regular encouragement and inspiration. My thanks also go to all the members of Calvary Bible Church for their love, encouragement and prayers.

Last, but not the least, I would like to extend my heartfelt gratitude to my sisters, Sandhya Thomas Singh, Vimmi Jacob and Aaradhana Ram Kashyap and their families for providing me with invaluable love, encouragement and prayers.

Foreword

Crowds never fascinated Jesus. Yet moved at their helplessness, he wept and in compassion he served them. He demanded of his disciples self-denial, love and service to God and humanity, especially to the poor and the downtrodden.

He modelled, as he washed the feet of his disciples, that any power that we may have is for the service of others. This utterly astonished his disciples! He cleansed the lepers and rehabilitated them to become participatory members of the society. By asking for a drink of water from a "Dalit" Samaritan woman he crossed the racial and sexual barriers, establishing new principles for social relationships.

The Church does not require larger-than-life leaders at helm, rather a community of disciples of Jesus, who translate creed into conduct, faith into practice and doctrine into daily living. No wonder Jesus began his ministry with a call to repentance. "Repent and believe in the good news" (Mark 1:15). Repenting is changing one's mind and direction. Jesus gave an object lesson on repentance when he placed a child among his disciples and said, "Unless you change and become like little children, you will never enter the kingdom of heaven." (Matt 18:3) He contrasted the trust and humility of a child with pride and self-seeking.

To be a disciple of Jesus requires spiritual formation regarding which Paul wrote: "Do not be conformed to this world, but be transformed by the renewal of your mind, that by testing you may discern what is the will of God, what is good and acceptable and perfect, (Romans 12:2)." Disciples are called not to conform to the patterns of behaviour and customs of this world, which are usually selfish and often corrupting. When the Holy Spirit renews, re-educates and redirects our minds, we are transformed.

More than a billion people on earth worship Jesus Christ as God incarnate. Some gladly live their faith commitments in very trying circumstances of suffering and martyrdom, while others overcome varied temptations of seductive materialism. However, the reality is all of us struggle with unconditional commitment to Christ as the Lord of our lives.

Jesus said, "You shall love the Lord your God with all your heart, and with all your soul, and with all your mind. This is the first and greatest commandment" (Mt. 22:37f). However, loving God is a gift from God and it must first of all be received. Paul writes, "God has poured out his love into our hearts by the Holy Spirit" (Romans 5:5). Loving God follows only from knowing God.

In our context when every creed is questioned and critiqued, it is imperative that the disciples of Jesus are equipped to give an answer when questioned. Otherwise Christian faith will be viewed as irrelevant. This indeed involves loving God with our mind.

Vikas Anand Ram has competently explored the role of the mind in growth and maturity in the disciples of Jesus Christ. The ultimate goal of discipleship is transformation into the likeness of Christ. I thank Vikas for exploring the theme of discipleship in the Scriptures, for the Church is called to disciple nations.

Rev. Dr. Richard Howell
General Secretary,
Evangelical Fellowhip of India (EFI) &
Asia Evegelical Alliance
New Delhi

Preface

India is known for its "gurus", "saints" and "swamis" who seek to provide their devotees with their blessings and solutions to life's problems. In such a context, words such as "disciple" or "discipleship" are, therefore, not unpopular. When Jesus began his earthy ministry, he called the twelve apostles (in addition to others) to be with him and to follow him. However, unlike all "gurus" and "swamis", Jesus did not promise a life full of riches, comforts and prosperity. On the contrary, Jesus warned his disciples in advance that because of him, they would be mistreated and persecuted (Jn. 15:18-21). Though it is true that Jesus promised his unending presence with his disciples, he did not want to paint a very rosy picture of the life with him. Discussing about the nature of discipleship, Jesus spoke that if anyone would like to follow him, he or she must deny him or herself, take up his or her cross and follow him daily (Lk.9:23-24). The Cross, as we all know, was a symbol of suffering and shame in the ancient world, as it stood as one of the cruelest and most humiliating forms of execution. So, it is not difficult to imagine that if someone was carrying his or her cross, they would not have gone downtown for shopping or for enjoying a gladiator's fight at the local stadium.

Jesus taught his disciples to make the pursuit of the Kingdom of God their highest priority (Matt. 6:33). The life of cross-bearing was, therefore, a call to die to all of ones' selfish ambitions and aspirations. This meant following Jesus wherever he led and giving up all other interests to the extent they became obstacles to this goal. Jesus made it clear to his disciples that following him meant serving others, just as he served others and gave his life for others (Mk. 10:43-45). Owing from the "wisdom tradition" of the Old Testament, Jesus is presented as the wisdom incarnate (Mt. 12:25-30, John's prologue). Thus, true wisdom is a "way of seeing", which attends to what lies hidden as well as to what lies on the surface, into which the disciples are given access through Jesus' invitation (Mt. 11:27-28).

These called-out disciples faced persecution by the world outside, but they also would have gone through struggles from within, as many of the things that Jesus did and taught appeared to be completely divorced and sometimes even opposed to their pre-existing Messianic framework and the larger Jewish socio-religious tradition. For instance, during one of the discourses, while Jesus spoke about his body as something to be eaten and blood as something to be consumed, many of his disciples were offended and decided to turn away from Jesus. At this, Jesus turns to his disciples and asks, "What about you? Do you also want to leave and go?" However, unlike the crowd, the disciples stick with Jesus and Peter, who stands out as a spokesman for the twelve, responds, "Where shall we go from you, for you have the words of life" (Jn. 6:68). This persistence was what differentiated the disciples from the rest of the crowd that followed Jesus.

Etymologically, "disciple" means a learner and, therefore, it has intellectual or academic connotations. The Gospels depict the disciples as those who were given the secret knowledge about the person of Jesus Christ (Mk. 4:9-10, Mt. 13:11, Lk. 8:9-10). Based on this revelation, Peter could confidently answer Jesus, when he asks them about his identity. Matthew records that after the disciples shared the popular perceptions regarding the person of Jesus, Jesus turned towards his disciples are asked, "But who do you say that I am?" At this Peter said, "You are Christ, the Son of the living God." To this Jesus responded that this truth (about his eternal identity) has not been revealed to them by flesh and blood (their own human knowledge) but by God, the Father from above (Matt. 16:17). However, even when the disciples have been given this knowledge about Lord Jesus Christ, they continue to falter in their understanding about Jesus' identity (and in turn theirs), his teachings and, at times, the symbolic meaning of his actions.

Mark, the earliest Gospel writer, depicts the disciples who constantly failed to understand Jesus' identity (Mk. 4:41, 6:51) and teachings about his passion (Mk. 8:32f, 9:10f, 32; 10:32). While Jesus talked about his impending betrayal, suffering and death, the disciples continuously failed to understand (9:18f, 28f, 33f; 10:13-16, 24, 26, 35ff). Similarly, the disciples also failed to understand the true nature of their own discipleship. While Jesus was about to enter Jerusalem, the brothers James and John put up a request before Jesus that they might sit on the two sides of Jesus, when he came to glory. In this the disciples failed to understand that glorification would be preceded by a painful period of suffering and death (about which Jesus had already been speaking – Mk. 10:33). However, the more serious level of misunderstanding was regarding the leadership structure of the Kingdom of God. Explaining again the upside-down leadership structure found in the Kingdom, Jesus told his disciples, "Whoever desires to become great among you shall be your servant…for the Son of Man did not come to be served, but to serve, and to give His life a ransom for many" (Mk. 10:43-45).

Matthew, on the other hand, portrays the disciples in a more positive light (Mt. 12:49-50). However, even when the disciples possess the gift of understanding in principle (13:11, 16-17) they continue to falter and fail and enter in conflict with Jesus. This is evident in their inability to trust him (during the storm in Mt. 8:23-27) and in their rejection of Jesus' words about his impending death and suffering (Mt. 16:22). According to Matthew, the chief difference between the disciples and the rest of the crowd is that even though they do not seem to understand Jesus' instructions and purpose in the beginning, at the end, they do understand and obey Jesus' instructions (Mt. 16:12; 17:13, 23; 28:17a). In contrast to the disciples, the crowds (13:10-17, 34-36) and the Jewish leaders ultimately reject Jesus, the Son of God (9:34; 12:14; 21:18-19, 41-43; 22:7; 23:37-39; 24:15; 27:25). In order to grow in discipleship, the disciples are exhorted to continue to apply their minds to understand Jesus' instructions in order to bear fruit for the kingdom of God (13:19a).

For Luke, the importance of understanding in discipleship is evident in that they are called to "count or reckon the cost" before committing to follow Jesus (Lk. 14:28-33). Positively, it meant loving God with all of one's heart, soul, strength and mind and one's neighbour as oneself (Lk. 10:27-28). Negatively, it meant saying "no" to all competing allegiances that sought to take the first place that only belongs to Jesus. However, for some it was an unjustified demand. For this reason, the rich man (Lk. 12:13-21) and the rich young ruler (Lk. 18:22-25) failed to enter into a life of discipleship (and thereby into eternal life). On the contrary, the disciples leave everything else to follow Jesus (Lk. 14:26-27, 33).

Even though the disciples had committed themselves to hearing and obeying his commands (Lk. 6:47-48 cf. v.20), they failed to understand the identity and purpose of Jesus (Lk. 8:25; 9:44-45; 18:31-34). The disciples continue to falter and fail to fully operate in the new paradigm that was revealed in Jesus. Thus, they argue about who was the greatest, vying for a higher position similar to how those in the world do (Lk. 9:46). Likewise, they aimed to be exclusive by forbidding an exorcist from casting out demons in Jesus' name (Lk. 9:49-50). In another instance, Jesus had to caution the disciples that their joy needed to be rightly placed, which is that their names have been written in the book of life and not that they have power over evil forces (Lk. 10:17-20). While entering into Jerusalem, the disciples begin to think that the kingdom would appear immediately (Lk. 19:11). In response to this, Jesus shared the parable of Talents, which revealed that the disciples are not so much called to look for final manifestation of the Kingdom as much as to faithfully execute the work entrusted to them. Even after Jesus' resurrection, the disciples continued to remain darkened regarding the full significance of the death of Jesus Christ. Jesus, however, enlightened them about the plan of salvation, so that they finally grasped the spiritual significance of Jesus' earthly ministry (Lk. 24:25-27, 44-45).

John presents Jesus as the creative "Word" through whom God created the universe. In doing so, he ascribes the role of "wisdom" to Jesus. Thus, just as in the case of "wisdom" in the Sapiential writings, in accepting and adhering to the words of Jesus, one enters into life and receives salvation. John operates on a dualistic worldview through utilising terms such as light and darkness, above and below, truth and falsehood. Humans belong to the "below" realm that is characterised by "darkness" and "lies." My mentor Dr. Cornelis calls it "epistemic darkness" that prevents people from understanding (Jn. 3:3; 8:23, 47; 9:24). However, this cannot be taken as an excuse by anyone for rejecting Jesus since sufficient evidence was available, which is needed to make a faith response (Jn. 3:19; 12:36-38; 14:11b; 15:24).

According to John, the incomprehension or misunderstanding of the disciples was primarily in three broad areas, namely the point of Jesus' identity (Jn. 1:38; 2:19-22; 4:10-11; 6:32-34) and teachings (Jn. 3:3-4; 11:12, 26-27; 12:15-17), the significance of Jesus' actions (13:7-13) and the passion and death of Jesus (Jn. 13:36-38; 16:18; 20:9). Through this portrayal of the disciples, John exhorts the readers to continue abiding in the words of Christ (8:31, 15:10) as only this guarantees ones fellowship with the Father and the Son (14:23). One of the reasons behind the progress of disciples is that they continually follow Jesus even when they do not fully understand (14:5-9, 16:17-18, 20:9). The crowd and the religious leaders, on the other hand, respond with hostility and unbelief to the teachings of Jesus. This indicates a willful refusal on the part of the world to accept the revelation brought by the Word (5:40; 8:27 cf. 8: 39, 43, 55; 10:38; 16:8-9; 18:38; 19:6).

John sees the Spirit as the "cognitive divine agent", one who enlightens human minds (Jn. 3:3f; 6:63; 14:17a). Since full bestowal of the Holy Spirit did not happen before the resurrection, a complete understanding of the mystery of Jesus Christ was only possible after Jesus had been glorified (16:13). After the earthly ministry of Jesus, the Spirit assumes the role of teacher, guiding the disciples into all truth and reminding them of the words of Jesus.

Down through history, people have attempted at finding answers that inform one's worldview with questions such as, What is truth? What is the meaning of life? It is important to ask questions simply because they help us to find their answers. Perhaps, that is why down through the ages, thinkers and philosophers have framed questions that would help us to construct a comprehensive paradigm for human life and conduct. For instance, Immanuel Kant in his *Critique of Pure Reason* came up with three basic questions, which every individual should ask in order to live a well-examined life. The questions are:

• What can I know?
• How do I decide what is right or wrong?
• What can I hope for or what is it I should be living for?

Let these questions keep ringing in your mind as you read this book. In this academic enquiry, I have adopted the narrative-critical method as the starting point in order to explore the author's implied meaning for the original audience. Similarly, looking at the *Sitz em leben* (original context), I have tried to discern the reasons behind the Gospel writers' distinctive emphases. Though this present work is not exhaustive, it is hoped that it would enable the reader to get a deeper insight into the dynamics of how human mind or cognitive abilities contribute to spiritual transformation through finding answers to issues that "really matter."

Rev. Vikas A. Ram
vikas.shalom@gmail.com

Abbreviations

Books of the Bible

Ge.	Genesis
Ex.	Exodus
Lev.	Leviticus
Nu.	Numbers
Dt.	Deuteronomy
Jos.	Joshua
Jdg.	Judges
Ru.	Ruth
1, 2 Sa.,	Samuel
1, 2 Ki.,	Kings
1, 2 Ch.,	Chronicles
Ezr.,	Ezra
Ne.,	Nehemiah
Est.,	Esther
Job	Job
Ps.,	Psalms
Pr.,	Proverbs
Ecc.,	Ecclesiastes
SS.,	Song of Solomon
Isa.,	Isaiah

Jer.,	Jeremiah
La.,	Lamentation
Eze.,	Ezekiel
Da.,	Daniel
Hos.,	Hosea
Joel	Joel
Am.,	Amos
Ob.,	Obadiah
Jnh.,	Jonah
Mic.,	Micah
Na.,	Nahum
Hab.,	Habbakuk
Zep.,	Zephaniah
Hag.,	Haggai
Zec.,	Zechariah
Mal.	Malachi
Mt.,	Matthew
Mk.,	Mark
Lk.	Luke
Jn.	John
Ac.,	Acts
Ro.,	Romans
1, 2 Co.,	Corinthians
Gal.,	Galatians
Eph.,	Ephesians
Php.,	Phillipians
Col.,	Colossians
1, 2 Th.,	Thessalonians
1, 2 Ti.,	Timothy
Tit.,	Titus
Phm.,	Philemon
Heb.,	Hebrew

Jas.,	James
1, 2 Pe.,	Peter
1, 2, 3 Jn.,	John
Jude	Jude
Rev.	Revelation

Other Works

ABD	Anchor Bible Dictionary
ABC	Anchor Bible Commentary
BECNT	Baker Exegetical Commentary on the New Testament
DJG	Dictionary of Jesus and the Gospels
IVP	InterVarsity Press
JBL	Journal of Biblical Literature
JSNT	Journal of the Study of the New Testament
JSNT Suppl. Ser.	Journal of the Study of the New Testament Supplementary Series
NICNT	The New International Commentary in the New Testament
NIGTC	The New International Greek Testament Commentary
NT	New Testament
NTS	New Testament Studies
NTT	New Testament Theology Series
OT	Old Testament
TDNT	Theological Dictionary of the New Testament
SBL Diss. Ser.	Society of Biblical Literature Dissertation Series
SBL Sem. Ser.	Society of Biblical Literature Semeia Series
SNTS	Society for New Testament Studies
Sir.	Sirach

SNTS Mon. Ser.	Society for New Testament Studies Monograph Series
SNTW	Society of the study of New Testament and its World
WBC	Word Biblical Commentary
Wisd.	Wisdom of Solomon

Introduction

I am a Christian and this makes me mightily concerned about the truths of the beliefs on which my commitment is built. If I cannot bring intellectual honesty to bear on my Christian beliefs, then those beliefs are fraud, for they claim to be true, not just dogmatic. On the other hand, if one can be both Christian and intellectual (sic?) honest, then Christianity will have a cognitive as well as emotional appeal.

—D. L. Wolfe[1]

We are living amidst technological advancements. It is an era when IT, BT and HT stands as hallmarks of human advancement.[2] This progress is possible as a result of humans having harnessed their intellectual capacities. As Christians, we actively participate in today's intellectually progressive era. However, usually we fail to apply our minds to our faith with the same intellectual rigor. Interestingly, such an attitude does not seem to trouble us, even as it contravenes the greatest commandment in the Bible: "Love the Lord your God with all your heart and with all your soul and with all your strength and with all your *mind*" (Mark 12:30 par. Mt.22:37; Lk.10:27). The present work is an attempt to explore the role of the mind in Christian life as portrayed in the Gospels.

We apply reason in our search for coherence and unity in our beliefs and avoid contradictions to make sense of our lives and surroundings. In the same way, reason is also important for thoughtful devotion and a reasonable faith. In fact, Jesus himself is a perfect example of the combination of perspicacious thought and Godly passion. Newman highlights the significance of the mind in matters of faith and views faith as "the *reasoning* of a divinely enlightened mind."[3]

Many consider doubt as the antithesis of faith, i.e., if you are a person of faith, you do not doubt anything at all and if you have doubts, you should feel guilty. It is clear that many do not realise the substantial role of reason and understanding as a means of scuffling with their doubts in Christian life. Therefore, they fail to experience constant spiritual growth. We are not and cannot really be honest individuals if we definitively avoid facing our doubts and queries. Tennyson succinctly expressed the above truth when he said, "There lives more faith in honest doubt, believe me, than in half the creeds."[4]

Although the subject of discipleship in the Gospels has been under much discussion, limited progress has been made about the role of the mind in discipleship. Thus, I believe there is an acute need for a fresh exploration of this specific facet of discipleship, as recorded in Gospel accounts.

In our present work, "mind" has been defined as the faculty of reason or cognition, will and emotions.[5] However, the present study will be primarily focusing on the first aspect of the mind, namely the role of the cognitive function of the mind in discipleship.

The term "disciple" has been defined as one who has committed him or herself to follow Jesus Christ as Lord, more from a logical and ingrained conclusion than merely a vow of personal devotion.

Although discipleship can be defined in different ways, we see discipleship as living a life in union with Jesus Christ (within a community), which seeks to grow in conformity to his image and to gain eternal rewards. It also includes the responsibility of discipling others.

Due to a large amount of commonality in the first three Gospels, there arises a question concerning their inter-relationship.

This problem of determining the inter-relationship among them is known as the "Synoptic Problem." It was first presented by Streeter (1924).[6] Since then, Markan priority has been most widely accepted among New Testament scholars. As per this theory, the Gospel of Mark is considered as the earliest written canonical Gospel. Stein undertook a major work to evaluate this theory and concluded that Markan priority is based not only on a single argument, but also on the cumulative weight of several arguments.[7]

Similarly, several other New Testament scholars have accepted Markan priority.[8] In accordance with the above scholars, Tuckett also examined the textual evidences and proposed that while the theory of Markan priority may not be without difficulties, it remains the most adequate solution to the so-called Synoptic Problem.[9]

The internal and external evidence[10] suggests that the Gospel of John is the last written canonical Gospel. Based on the above premises, we have undertaken the present study beginning with the Gospel of Mark and followed by the Gospels of Matthew, Luke and John.

I have attempted to present the history of scholarship based on the Gospels.

Role of the Mind in Markan Discipleship
Marshall sees Markan discipleship as a constant oscillation between the values and outlook of the "unbelieving generation" and those values prescriptive of God's rule. He sees that Mark portrays the disciples as examples out of his pastoral concern.[11] Marshall sees the disciples as different from the Jewish leaders,[12] because the disciples do not reject the truth.[13] Marshall looks at the textual evidence and argues that it points to the disciples' misunderstanding.

Initially, Mark presents the disciples in a positive light. However, their negative portrait begins from 4:13f onwards. Gradually, their failure of understanding is obvious in their inability to understand Jesus' words (4:13; 5:31; 6:37; 7:18; 8:4, 15f) and miracles (4:38ff; 6:52; 8:19-21). Marshall says that this incomprehension is because the disciples fail to understand Jesus' true identity (4:41; 6:51). They also did not understand Jesus' teaching about his passion (8:32f; 9:10f, 32; 10:32) and of their own discipleship (9:18f, 28f, 33f; 10:13-16, 24, 26, 35ff).[14] Thus, according to Marshall, the real cause of the disciples' failure is not so much a willful rejection of the truth (volitional) as their failure to translate their intuitive insights about Jesus' significance into a fuller understanding of Jesus' identity and mission.[15] In this way, Marshall sees the inaptitude of the disciples as the basic cause for the disciples' constant failures.[16] Marshall considers 14:38 ("The spirit is willing but the body is weak") as the disciples' evaluative summary.[17] Thus, Marshall points to the vital role of the cognitive function of the mind in Markan discipleship.

Wilkins sees discipleship as fundamentally a master and disciple relationship.[18] Wilkins says that Mark wrote to his community about disciples' failure[19] intentionally to instruct his readers of how difficult it is to grasp the mystery of Jesus and the Cross.[20] According to Wilkins, "servanthood" is the key issue of the disciples' incomprehension.

Wilkins sees that the disciples' responses represent one of the dominant themes[21] through which Mark depicts heavenly and earthly viewpoints.[22] On the one hand, the disciples were commissioned with the authority of Jesus (1:16-20; 3:13-19) and heard the secrets of the kingdom of God (4:10-12), but on the other, they did not understand the mystery of Jesus (4:13; 7:17-18; 4:35-41; 6:45-52; 6:34-44; 8:1-10; 8:14-21).[23]

Wilkins also highlights that the theme about the inaptitude of the disciples is clearly evident in placing the two passages (9:33-37 and 10:35-45)[24] within the larger section of the Markan discipleship discourse (8:27- 10:45). Mark sees the identity and mission of Jesus and his summons to "servanthood" as key points of the disciples' incomprehension. Wilkins thus sees the human limitation as the cause for the disciples' incomprehension. And his reading of Mark projects the vital role of the cognitive function of the mind in discipleship.

Rhoads, Dewey and Michie view the healing of the blind man in stages, as symbolic of the progressive understanding of the disciples.[25] The authors contend that Mark uses the motif of "misunderstanding" as a literary device by which he reveals Jesus' standard for discipleship.[26]

The authors also evince a gradual development in the understanding of the disciples in the Markan plot.[27] In the beginning of the plot, the disciples remain at Jesus' side, following his instructions. However, the authors observe that later, Mark portrays the disciples as having difficulty in following Jesus, due to their lack of understanding and fear.[28] Throughout the text (especially 6:45-52 and 9:32), the authors identify fear and lack of understanding as a vicious cycle of cause and effect: fear inhibits understanding and misunderstanding generates fear.[29] The authors ascribe the disciples' incomprehension to their fear as well as to their inability of grasping the mindset of faith.[30]

At the mid-point of the Markan narrative, Rhoads and others view a thematic shift from a lack of understanding to misunderstanding.[31] It is because of this misunderstanding that Peter rebukes Jesus when he speaks about his impending death and resurrection. The authors see that though the disciples accept Jesus as the anointed one, they still continue to share the cultural expectations of their time about the promised Messiah.[32] Nevertheless, the disciples "see" clearly enough to "follow him" to Jerusalem.[33]

At Jerusalem, the disciples fail to grasp their own frailty when they were face to face with death.[34] Rhoads and others contend that Peter's grief over his failure also opened a possibility for the disciples to "turn around" and follow.[35] At the end, the authors see that Mark aimed to raise the following questions for his readers: "What will you do when faced with death and persecution for the Good News? Can you remain faithful? And if you fail can you begin again?"[36] Thus, while the authors see "incomprehension" as an important theme for Mark, unlike Wilkins and Marshall, they also see a willing disposition and faith as the remedy for the disciples' incomprehension.

Riches points out that 8:22-26 and 10:46-52 (the two narratives concerning blind men) form an *inclusio* which bracket the passages on discipleship and the Cross.[37] Like Rhoads and others, Riches argues that the healing of the blind men provides a clue to understanding the new life of a believer; wherein, like the healing of the blind in stages (8:22-26), illumination to a disciple may not come all at once but in stages gradually.[38]

Riches attests that Mark highlights two views of discipleship: firstly, where the disciples are forged haltingly and with misunderstanding and failure into a new community;[39] and secondly, where they are called out for a special task of proclaiming and ushering in the kingdom of God.[40] Riches opines that Mark sees that the disciples' lives show an adequate evidence for lack of understanding (4:13; 6:52; 8:4, 17-21) and faith (4:40; 6:50).[41] Riches attributes the above frailty of the disciples to the radically corrupt human nature. And he asserts that the frequent failures of the disciples underline the need for self-discipline within the Markan community.[42] Thus, Riches argues that Mark's focus is to show the ultimate struggle of the human "will" for renewal and restoration and observes Markan emphasis on "choice" and "high demands" that are expected from the followers.[43] Only those who *choose* to follow Jesus will be led [passive] to the truth of the new world in which they have entered.[44]

On the basis of 3:20-25, Riches observes that Mark defines the true family of Jesus as those who do the "will of God" as Jesus teaches it.[45] Riches argues that the remedy for this failure lies in faithfulness to and in understanding the mystery of the kingdom of God, into which they have been initiated.[46] Thus, Riches sees a limited role of the cognitive function of the mind in Markan discipleship, as he argues that Mark lays emphasis on human "choice" and discipline.

In our review of the above scholarly works, all scholars agree regarding the significant place of the theme of "incomprehension" in Mark. However, their view differs as to its cause and remedy. Marshall and Wilkins see the disciples' inaptitude as a major deterrent to the disciples' incomprehension. Thus, the remedy is to apply one's mind to overcome the incomprehension. Rhoads and others see fear and lack of faith as the cause of the disciples' incomprehension. Thus, in their view, Mark exhorts his readers to practice faith and commit themselves to Jesus in order to overcome incomprehension. In this sense, they do not see the cognitive function of the mind as significant in overcoming incomprehension. Riches agrees with Marshall and Wilkins regarding the cause of disciples' incomprehension. However, he sees "human volition" as the crucial factor, which needs renewal, as it plays a vital role in overcoming incomprehension. Unlike all others, Riches also sees that in Mark the role of the cognitive function of the mind comes into play only for those who have a willing and open disposition to Jesus and his instructions.

Role of the Mind in Matthean Discipleship

Luz states that unlike Mark, Matthew reveals that while the disciples initially fail to understand,[47] they *do* understand after Jesus' instructions.[48] Luz says that this picture of the disciples[49] is not contrary to the Markan portrait, rather it is a supplement to it. This is because in Matthew, unlike Mark, the disciples have gained an understanding about Jesus' being and the focus of their understanding is shifted to his teachings.[50] Since the disciples understand Jesus' teachings, Luz enunciates that for Matthew, "understanding" is the prerequisite for a Christian life and teaching. In other words, understanding is the prerequisite to be a *faithful* Christian.[51] This implies that growth in discipleship is only possible when one understands Jesus' teachings. Luz continues to say that Matthew presupposes that the disciples already understand, when he sees discipleship as doing the "will of God" in 12:50.[52] Thus, for Luz, Matthew clearly emphasises the role of the cognitive function of the mind in discipleship.

Kingsbury views the story of the disciples as a sub-theme in the story of Jesus.[53] He notes that though people come to Jesus solely on God's initiative (as the disciples are recipients of divine revelation, 11:2-16:20), this coming is based on a reasoned choice.[54]

Kingsbury highlights that (though the disciples possess the gift of understanding in principle, 13:11, 16-17, 51),[55] the disciples are in conflict with Jesus, which gradually intensifies at the end of the Matthean plot.[56] The author sees this conflict as the disciples falter (evident in the storm event in 8:23-27) and fail badly at times (evident in 16:22, 17:14-20), even when they are open-minded and aspire to appropriate Jesus' evaluative point of view.[57]

Kingsbury sees that the conflict is not primarily in regard to their perception about Jesus' identity, but in adopting his evaluative point of view as servanthood.[58] He argues that through the conflicts and differences, Jesus aimed to instruct his disciples or to mediate to them insight or perception.[59] Kingsbury says that finally, at the end of the third section, the disciples understand that suffering Sonship is a summons to suffering discipleship.[60]

Thus, Kingsbury emphasises the role of the cognitive function of the mind as a remedy for overcoming conflict with Jesus. The conflict was not principally because the disciples were unwilling to follow Jesus, but because time and again they failed to gain a fuller insight into Jesus' ministry and its implications for them.

Wilkins says that Matthew through his Gospel aims to present the fulfillment of God's redeeming activity in Jesus.[61] Wilkins has identified two main aims of Matthew's Gospel. First aim is to accentuate Jesus and his teachings.[62] He fulfills this aim by emphasising that the true disciples understand Jesus' teachings.[63] The second aim is to emphasise that the true disciples are only those whom Jesus instructs, and who in turn instruct others.[64]

Commenting upon Matthean discipleship, Wilkins observes that Matthew emphasises that the essence of true discipleship lies in understanding and obeying Jesus' teaching.[65] Wilkins views the command to "teach" (in the Great Commission) as the activity that includes not only instruction, but also obedience to Jesus' commands.[66] Wilkins observes that Matthew portrays true disciples as those who grow in discipleship by obeying the master's instruction.[67] Again while summarising his chapter, Wilkins says that obedience to Jesus' teaching is the core of discipleship training.[68] Wilkins observes that though it is important to understand the teachings of Jesus (as understanding is the mark of true disciples), Matthew lays an equal emphasis on obedience, as it proves their true comprehension. Thus, Wilkins sees the role of both the cognitive as well as the volitional function of the mind as vital for discipleship in Matthew.

Riches says that Matthew operates under two broad mythological schemata:

* The *revolutionist response*, which sees that God must intervene in the end to sweep away the present evil age.

* The *reformist response*, which sees that the world will be set right when the people who have accepted God's teaching are forgiven and follow Him along the way.[69]

Riches sees that Matthew lays more importance on the human responsibility in God's overall plan of salvation.[70] Therefore, in the Gospel according to Matthew, people must accept Jesus' call and teaching. They must learn to do the will of God to become Jesus' brothers and sisters.[71] Riches contends that for Matthew, discipleship is a call into a teaching and healing community, where ultimately the teaching ministry is of the greatest importance.[72] Riches' observes that Matthew emphasises on "volition" as he views those outside the community, who choose to remain under the cloud of ignorance.[73] Riches see a similar emphasis in Jesus' teaching and in the Great Commission.[74] Thus, where Mark presents discipleship as transition from darkness to light (in the healing of the blind in stages Mk. 8:21-26), Matthew presents discipleship as a call to membership within a community of faith, schooled in Jesus' teaching.[75] This requires an initial choice and a continual application of one's cognitive abilities to understand and obey Jesus' instruction. According to Riches, an exercise of the human will is critical for admission to the ranks of discipleship; it is equally vital to make an effort to learn Jesus' teachings. Thus, he points to the important role of the cognitive and volitional aspects of the mind as crucial for understanding and discipleship.

In our overview of Matthean scholarship, scholars agree that in Matthew the disciples understand Jesus and his instructions. Luz and Kingsbury place strong emphasis on the cognitive function of the mind as crucial for discipleship. He points to the areas of the disciples' conflict with Jesus and sees the important need of the disciples to apply their cognitive abilities to resolve the conflict. Both Wilkins and Riches emphasise the need for activity of the human will as well as for cognition in understanding Jesus' instruction. However, Wilkins sees the volitional function of the mind as of greater import, as it is obedience to Jesus' instruction that proves true comprehension.

Role of the Mind in Lukan Discipleship

Doohan says Luke wrote his Gospel for a community that was continuously under criticism.[76] These criticisms were from forces that were undermining the confidence in the future of the "Way" and had cast doubt on the truth concerning "the things of which they were instructed."[77] Luke asserts that the vision of human life that Jesus brings is not attained through acquiring knowledge but through active participation.[78] The commitment of each disciple must not only be to understanding Jesus' words, but also to obeying Jesus' teachings.[79] Thus, discipleship is built on the foundation of obedience (e.g., the wise and foolish builder in 6:47). For Luke, true understanding is proved only through obedience and obedience, in turn, facilitates further understanding.

Doohan sees Luke's vision of the Twelve in a positive light as they carry on the ministering work of the Lord[80] and remain *with Jesus*, even at the time of his suffering (22:49).[81] In Luke and Acts, no one earns discipleship and usually those who are the best candidates by human standards[82] are not ready for the Lord's call.[83] Doohan argues that Luke emphasises that following Jesus is a lifetime commitment and, therefore, conversion is an ongoing reality and is indistinguishable from discipleship.[84]

The chief discipleship section is 9:51-19:27.[85] It contains complex teachings that needs explanation, because the disciples need a clearer understanding about Jesus' mission and teachings.[86]

Furthermore, Luke views discipleship as a difficult challenge and asserts that one should not make hasty decisions regarding it, but rather "count the cost" of discipleship.[87] This points to the importance of the cognitive function of the mind in discipleship. Doohan observes that the disciples "slowly" became ready for commissioning (22: 44-49).[88] He says that even when the disciples were with Jesus with an obedient attitude, they did not easily realise Jesus' perspective. This implies that the struggle for the disciples was not primarily because of a willful ignorance, but because of their inability to understand. Thus, Doohan points to the disciples' inaptitude as the cause behind their incomprehension. In Doohan's view, Luke highlights the cognitive and volitional functions of the mind as crucial for overcoming incomprehension.

On the basis of Acts 20:25-28,[89] Beck, in line with Doohan, sees that Luke's purpose was to summon the post-apostolic church back to the standards of its founding era.[90] To this end, Luke depicts various characters as model disciples.[91] Based on 22:67, Beck observes that the basic disposition of faith involves the assent of the human will (cf. 20:5; Acts 5:32).[92] Similarly, in the stilling of the storm in 8:25, Beck sees an example of the need for constant faith after an initial response (8:13).[93] In Luke, discipleship is set in the context of commitment to Jesus on his journey.[94] Like Matthew, Luke also emphasises the need to be schooled in the teachings of Jesus, if obedience (upon which he lays equal stress) is to follow.[95] Through Peter's example, Luke shows that promises are easy to make but the cost must be counted in advance (cf. 14:28f).[96] Beck also sees Mary as a model disciple, who unlike others, kept pondering about the shepherds visitation in her heart (2:19 cf. 2:51).[97] Beck contends through Mary's example that Luke lays stress on the need for understanding.[98] However, gaining such an understanding is not so easy, which is evident from 2:35 and 2:48-51.[99] Thus, Beck argues that Luke intended to highlight the difficulty of the disciples for understanding Jesus' journey to Jerusalem.[100]

Luke sees Mary as a positive example (2:51). Mary keeps pondering about the meaning of events (2:19), seeking the understanding she does not yet have. Thus, Beck sees the disciples' difficulty to understand Jesus' identity and mission as the reason for the disciples' conflict and incomprehension. Beck thus, argues that in Luke, the remedy for incomprehension lies in a willing disposition and in applying one's cognitive abilities to understand Jesus' instruction.

Kingsbury sees the disciples as models who falter and, at times, do not serve the purposes of God, but of humans.[101] The root of the problem lies in the incomprehension of the disciples concerning God's plan of salvation in Jesus.[102] Kingsbury sees incomprehension as the cause of spiritual immaturity of the disciples.[103] It is precisely because of the disciples' incomprehension that Jesus struggles to explain his mission to them.

Even though the disciples are "enlightened" (for they are the recipients of divine revelation, 10:21-24, and of the mysteries of God's kingdom, 8:10) and obedient,[104] they fail to comprehend completely Jesus' point of view.[105] Luke highlights that only in the end do the disciples understand the saving purposes of God in Jesus (24:44-45). Thus, only at the end, the disciples become ready to undertake the worldwide ministry Jesus had in store for them (24:44-49). Also, it is at this moment, that the disciples are able to understand the essential truth about discipleship as "servanthood."[106]

Pointing to the cause of the disciples' incomprehension, Kingsbury says, "On one hand, the disciples are themselves at fault for not comprehending...on the other, it belongs to God's purposes that the disciples do not comprehend Jesus' passion." He goes on to say, "Whatever the tension, each part must be given its due."[107] Thus, Kingsbury points to the crucial role of the cognitive function of the mind in Lukan discipleship.

Green says that Luke presents discipleship[108] through the "journey motif,"[109] as following "the Way"(Acts 18:24-25; cf. e.g., Luke 1:6; 20:21).[110] He sees that discipleship is possible only because of God's gracious intervention in human affairs.[111] Green argues that according to Luke, because of the danger of apostasy (cf. 8:12) "faith" is an ongoing need for discipleship.[112] Green says that the word "repentance" is not widely used in Luke, but the concept is ubiquitous and means redirecting one's heart and life towards the purposes of God.[113]

Green observes that initially the disciples fail to understand Jesus' being.[114] This is evident in their response of fear and amazement in the sea storm event (8:22-25).[115] Later, the feeding miracles were effective to elicit Peter's confession of Jesus as the God's Messiah in 9:18-20.[116] Thus, Green sees the role of Peter's cognitive ability behind his confession. However, even after the confession, Peter (and the disciples) still shows his lack of understanding (e.g. 9:33) and immaturity.[117] Green comments that in Luke, true discipleship involves not only calling Jesus "Lord, Lord", but it also signifies "hearing and obeying" (cf. 8:21; 10:38-42; 11:27-28).[118] Thus, radical obedience becomes the order for true discipleship (12:35-48; cf. 13:24-27; 17:7-10).[119]

Green observes that Luke calls the disciples to "count the cost" of discipleship before entering the journey (14:25-33).[120] Green points out that although obedience is ultimately vital for discipleship, progress in discipleship also depends upon comprehending the things of God. Thus, Green points to the role of the cognitive function of the mind in overcoming incomprehension.

In the above overview on Lukan discipleship, all four Lukan scholars lay an emphasis on the importance of the cognitive function of the mind. Kingsbury also goes to answer the reason for the disciples' incomprehension. All the four scholars discussed above observe the Lukan emphasis on the need to apply one's cognitive and volitional abilities to overcome incomprehension.

Role of the Mind in Johannine Discipleship

Collins observes that John's Gospel can be read at two levels. The first level is the literal (in which the evangelist narrates the tale of

Jesus of Nazareth in almost a matter-of-fact fashion) and sensory. The second is the cognitive or spiritual, in which the evangelist tells the story of the Johannine community, its faith and its struggles.[121] Collins observes that the calling of the first disciples (1:35-39) laid the foundation for John's account of discipleship.[122] He observes four key words from the call narrative that presents a paradigm for Johannine discipleship. They are: following, seeking, seeing and staying.[123]

John makes use of the words "to follow"[124] to depict a disciple's life.[125] Thus, a true disciple is one who follows Jesus. The words "to seek" is Jesus' first speech in the Gospel (1:38)[126] through which Jesus challenges people to search him[127] because only those who search him are his true disciples.[128] Collins continues to argue that John represent Mary Magdalene as a model disciple who searches for Jesus and subsequently Jesus manifests himself to her.[129] Thus, Collins sees a strong Johannine emphasis on searching, which is principally a cognitive activity.

In the same way, "to see" refers to the appreciation of the true reality, which is possible only on Jesus' invitation.[130] Since the two verbs ἰδεῖν and ὁραν are used interchangeably, Collins argues that real seeing is one that is accompanied by understanding.[131]

"To stay" symbolically means a permanent abode. Collins observes that the disciples, not fully aware of Jesus' eternal abode, ask Jesus, "Where are you staying?"[132] However, later readers from a post-resurrection perspective come to know that Jesus abides forever (12:34).[133]

Supporting the importance of the cognitive function of the mind in John's Gospel, Collins observes questioning as an important activity (2:3-4; 2:18-19; 3:4-5 etc.). Based on 1:38, He argues that in John only true comprehension of Jesus' being can make discipleship possible.[134] Collins further contends that this understanding comes only by being in relationship with Jesus.[135] Thus, Collins states that true disciples are those who genuinely seek to know Jesus' true identity. And because Jesus reveals himself to them, they are led into discipleship.

In this way, Collins sees a very strong emphasis on the role of the cognitive aspect of the mind in Johannine discipleship. This is clear, as without understanding true discipleship is an impossibility. He argues that adequate understanding about Jesus' identity and mission was possible for the disciples in the pre-Easter period. However, he does not explore the reason behind the disciples' incomprehension.

Smith argues that the disciples did not and could not have had a *complete* understanding of Jesus' identity until his death and resurrection.[136] Thus, while the disciples truly believed in Jesus, (2:11; 6:67-68) and followed him (11:16), they could not have understood him fully. This becomes apparent in the end of Jesus' farewell discourse (16:31f).[137]

Smith also identifies the theme of misunderstanding in John, and argues that it emphasises that no one can truly understand Jesus on his or her own terms. Though the disciples understand Jesus' being to some extent,[138] true comprehension comes only when the Holy Spirit helps them to understand Jesus' being as the divine Logos (Jn.20:20) after resurrection.[139] According to Smith, fuller discipleship is possible when one through the Holy Spirit comprehends Jesus as the divine 'Logos'.

Smith also argues for a Johannine emphasis on the need of understanding Jesus' being for growth in discipleship. Thus, there is an implicit emphasis on the role of the cognitive aspect of mind in discipleship. Regarding the reason of the disciples' misunderstanding, Smith sees it as a result of their unique situation before the Cross.

Kostenberger says that the disciples play an important part in the journey to Jerusalem (cf. 9:2; 11:7-16, 54; 12:16, 21-22), where they follow Jesus.[140] He sees the twelve in a positive light.[141] In contrast to the crowd, who follows only externally (6:2, 5, 22, 24), without understanding, (cf. 11:42; 12:29, 43) and also characterised by unbelief (a closed heart, 12:36b-41), the disciples follow Jesus with faith and understanding.[142] At the same time, the disciples' misunderstandings are repeatedly emphasised in John's Gospel.[143]

Like Smith, Kostenberger also argues that through the disciples' misunderstandings, John seems to emphasise the work of the Holy Spirit, who gives understanding (2:22; 12:16).[144] Kostenberger also holds that the incomprehension of the disciples is due to their inaptitude. Thus, he sees a clear emphasis on the role of the cognitive function of the mind in discipleship.

Bennema also sees that though the disciples apparently had an adequate understanding and belief, they did not cognitively perceive everything that Jesus tried to teach them (14:5-9; 16:17-18; 20:9; cf. 6:5-7).[145] Bennema also argues that adequate understanding (which is indispensable for saving faith) was possible before the Cross.[146] Regarding the chief object of comprehension, Bennema sees it as the knowledge of God's doings as revealed in and through Jesus. This knowledge is vital as it is the basis of fellowship with the Father (15:15).[147] He sees that such a knowledge is mediated through the Holy Spirit, who continues to lead the disciples to a higher level of cognitive perception (14:26; 16:12-15), which is vital for the disciples' continuous belief and *to sustain* them in discipleship (2:22).[148]

The author sees salvation as an ongoing event, in terms of understanding and accepting the "saving truth" of Jesus' teaching.[149] More than the synoptic Gospels, the fourth Gospel emphasises human responsibility in one's salvation, which is clear as the main reason for people's unbelief is found in people themselves (3:19-20).[150]

Bennema goes to argue that discipleship requires continuously[151] remaining[152] in Jesus' teaching (8:31), as only this guarantees one's fellowship with the Father and the Son (14:23; 2Jn. 9).[153] On another occasion, Bennema sees bearing fruit in John 15 as a test for discipleship that can be passed or failed, depending upon whether one remains in Jesus or not (Bennema, 140). Since one can only remain in Jesus through knowing and obeying his teachings, it implies that in bearing fruit and thereby in discipleship, both human cognition and volition play a role.

The importance of the cognitive element in John is evident as Jesus' main activity in John's Gospel is teaching (6:59; 7:14-17, 28; 8:2, 20; 18:19-20).[154] Jesus' teachings are soteriologically oriented as they reveal that God-acceptance (1:18; 3:12-13) sets one free from sins (8:31-36).[155] Here, the author clearly emphasises the role of the cognitive aspect of mind in discipleship.

Regarding "knowing" and "doing" in salvation discipleship, Bennema sees that as the disciple moves in obedience with the available understanding, she or he remains in fellowship with the Father (3:21; 1Jn.1:6-7). And by being in fellowship with the Father, a disciple, in turn, comes to perceive further truth (8:31-33) aided by the Spirit of Truth (16:13; cf. 1Jn. 5:6).[156]

Bennema again points to the importance of the cognitive role of the mind in discipleship when he observes that though "hearing" and "seeing" are important for salvation, they do not automatically lead one to salvation, which is possible only when they lead to cognitive perception[157.158] Thus, in the end, Bennema points us to a clear Johannine emphasis on the cognitive aspect of the mind in discipleship.[158]

In our discussion of the four key scholars, all of them clearly present an emphasis on the role of the cognitive aspect of the mind in Johannine discipleship. Bennema uniquely argues that adequate understanding was possible for making a saving belief response. Scholars differ regarding the cause of the disciples' incomprehension or misunderstanding. However, there is a clear impression from the discussed scholars that John's reading largely sees human cognition as indispensable for discipleship.

Statement of the Problem

In the above discussion on discipleship from the Gospels, we have observed that the disciples struggled while they followed Jesus. We also observed that the scholars do not entirely agree on the reason for the disciples' incomprehension. Though the scholars have discussed the theme of incomprehension, they have not adequately examined the role of the mind in discipleship. They have also not dealt with the concept of the mind and the heart in the Gospel tradition. The above discussion shows the gaps in Gospel studies with respect to the role of the mind. This opens up a need for a fresh understanding of the concept of the mind and its role in discipleship in Gospel narratives. Due to the limitation of our study, I will be focusing mainly on the role of the cognitive function of the mind, which pertains to understanding.

Aim

The aim is to explore the role of the cognitive function of the mind in discipleship in the Gospels. This would enable us to see how the cognitive aspect of the mind facilitates growth and maturity in discipleship.

Key Questions

The present work aims to answer the following questions:

• Can people know God?

• What is the concept of discipleship in the Gospels?

• What is the concept of the "mind" in the Gospel tradition?

• What are the causes and remedies of the disciples' incomprehension?

• What is the role of the cognitive function of the mind in discipleship?

Methodology

The present study aims to examine the four Gospels in order to trace the role of the cognitive function of the mind in discipleship. In this study, I have worked with the following presuppositions:

• Based on Markan priority, I assume that Mark is the earliest written Gospel. Therefore, we have begun our study with the Gospel of Mark.

• All the four Gospels were written as purely historical accounts (the historicising approach[159]), but they also address specific needs of their respective communities (transparency approach[160]), which is also why they present different discipleship emphases.[161]

It is precisely for this reason that each chapter begins with a brief discussion on the respective communities and discipleship portrait sketched by the four evangelists. This is followed by an examination of the nature of the each Gospel. This follows study on the evangelists' epistemological framework. This helps us to discover the source and object of knowledge and process of knowing according to each evangelist. This follows a discussion on the purpose of disciples' incomprehension. Exploring the theme of disciples' incomprehension follows this. Each chapter concludes with a discussion on how each evangelist's epistemological framework might have possibly influenced their communities. For the sake of convenience, I will be using the term "understanding" to denote the cognitive function of the mind.

Scope and Limitation

The four Gospels will be the primary source of inquiry, as they have not been adequately explored in relation to the role of the mind in discipleship. This means that I will only focus on the role of the cognitive function of the mind in the lives of those who are already disciples of Christ. I have not studied Gospel accounts from a philosophical perspective or looked at the dynamics of how a person is saved.

End Notes

[1] Quoted in Cornelis Bennema, "What has Athens to Do with Jerusalem? A Study of Johannine Epistemology," *Bible and Epistemology*, (eds.) R. Perry and M. Healy (Carlisle: Paternoster, forthcoming, 2006).

[2] IT, BT and HT stands for Information Technology, Bio-Technology and Health Technology respectively.

[3] Cheryl Clemons, "Loving God With the Mind - Christian Discipleship and the Role of the Intellect: Insight from John Henry Newman." *www.umass.edu/catholic/campus/conf/LovingGodWiththeMind. doc*; (Accessed on June 07, 2004).

[4] *http://www.annabelle.net/topics/author.php?firstname=Lord&lastname= Tennyson*; (Accessed on June 08, 2004).

[5] The Little Oxford English Dictionary. 8th edn. ed. Angus Stevenson with Julia Elliot and Richard Jones (Oxford: Oxford University Press, 2002), 440.

[6] C.M. Tuckett, "Synoptic Problem," in *ABD*, ed. David Noel Freedman, vol. 6 (New York: Doubleday, 1992), 264.

[7] See Robert H. Stein. *The Synoptic Problem: An Introduction* (Nottingham: IVP, 1988), 45-86. They are the argument from length, from grammar, from verbal agreements and order, from literary agreements, from redaction, and from Mark's more primitive theology.

[8] Riches, *The Synoptic Gospels*, 59; Kostenberger, *Encountering John*, 98; Nelson, *Leadership and Discipleship*, 13; Aarry Smith, "Jesus as Teacher in Synoptic Gospels." http://www.abu.nb.ca/Courses/NTIntro/LifeJ/TeacherJesus.htm; (accessed on July 15, 2004).

[9] C.M. Tuckett, "Synoptic" in *ABD*, vol. 6, 268.

[10] Their evidence is dealt in brief with in Chapter Five.

[11] Christopher D. Marshall, Faith *as a Theme in Mark's Narrative* (Cambridge: Cambridge Press, 1989), 223.

[12] He views two passages (4:35-41 and 9:14-29) that focus exclusively at the disciples, and which are parts of the motif of 'discipleship failure' in Mark's gospel.

[13] Marshall, *Faith*, 210. Even when the disciples show lack of faith (Mk. 4:40-41), and do not seem to understand Jesus' words (Mk. 4:13), Marshall sees them as different from the Jewish authorities, who willfully seek to oppose Jesus and his teachings (Marshall, *Faith*, 213).

[14] Marshall, *Faith*, 209.

[15] *Ibid.*, 225.

[16] In addition, he also shows that the cognitive defect obviously has a volitional component. This is clear from the 'shock tactics' Jesus employs to jolt the disciples out of their spiritual myopia (which at times, appears to work cf. 8:17-21 and 8:27-30) (Marshall, *Faith*, 225).

[17] Marshall, *Faith*, 211.

[18] Michael J. Wilkins, *Following the Master* (Grand Rapids, Michigan: Zondervan, 1992), 172.

[19] *Ibid.*, 199. Wilkins asserts that though Mark had a very high regard for the disciples, he uses them as negative examples to instruct the community about the necessity of thinking the thoughts of God rather than the thoughts of humans (8:33). (*Ibid.*, 200).

[20] *Ibid.*, 199.

[21] *Ibid.*, 197.

[22] *Ibid.*, 196. For these viewpoints, Wilkins uses the terms *'thinking the things of God'* and *'thinking the things of humankind'*.

[23] *Ibid.*, and sometimes, for e.g. 6:52, it seems that they behaved like the Pharisees, whose hearts were hardened, which was more of a volitional act rather than cognitive.

[24] In these two instances, Jesus' disciples misunderstood the motive and nature of his ministry in terms of suffering servanthood and the cross.

[25] David Rhoads, Johanna Dewey, and Donald Michie, *Mark as a Story*, 2nd ed. (Minneapolis: Fortress, 1999), 126.

[26] *Ibid.*, 123.

[27] *Ibid.*, 124.

[28] *Ibid.*, The Authors illustrate this as the disciples do not see (understand) the full possibilities of the rule of God at several points: in storm at sea, in the desert without food etc. They are also frightened by the storm, by Jesus' power to calm sea, by his walking over the water and anxious about the lack of bread. *Ibid.*, 125.

[29] The Authors illustrate it through the text. When Jesus mentions about his coming persecution and death, they did not understand and were afraid to ask him (9:32). On the occasion of sea storm event (6:45-52), fear of well being prevented them from understanding.

[30] David Rhoads, *Mark as a Story*, 126.

[31] *Ibid.*, 125. The Authors see this misunderstanding that leads them to a state of fear as Mark says , 'those who followed were afraid.' They go on to illustrate that the disciple's fear kept them from understanding as Mark says, 'For they did not understand what he said and they were all afraid to ask him,' *Ibid.*, 126.

[32] *Ibid.*, 92.

[33] *Ibid.*, 126.

[34] *Ibid.*, 127. Mark portrays the disciples as giving the last word rather than Jesus, which the authors suggest was a construction to show the self-sufficient attitude of the disciples, (*Ibid.*, 94). Authors also see that through the disciples' failings at Gethsemane, Mark parallels them to the seed falling on the rocky ground. Though the hearers may have had an high opinion about the word 'rock', but Mark uses it negatively in the parable of Sower, which suggests a different and ironic meaning to the name. This complies well with Mark's portrayal of the disciples as those having a hard (dull) mind and those who do not easily understand. (*Ibid.*, 128).

[35] *Ibid.*, 127.

[36] *Ibid.*, 128.

[37] John K. Riches, *Conflicting Mythologies: Identity Formation in the Gospel of Mark and Matthew*, SNTW (Edinburgh: T&T Clark, 2000), 69.

[38] *Ibid.*, 72.

[39] A community of those, who have abandoned their old attachments of community (kinship, customs, land and cultic sites) and have found a new family in the company and following of Jesus.

[40] Riches, *Conflicting*, 87.

[41] *Ibid.*, 73.

[42] *Ibid.*, 146. This is why they are unable to understand God's mysteries on their own. Consequently, the receiving of sight (understanding) is only partially under human control and essentially remaining as a gift. (*Ibid.*, 82).

[43] This choice entailed loosing one's life (8:34-38) and thinking the things of God (8:33). *Ibid.*, 92.

[44] *Ibid.*, 69.

[45] *Ibid.*, 77.

[46] *Ibid.*, 81.

[47] Ulrich Luz, "The Disciples in the Gospel according to Matthew," in *The Interpretation of Matthew*, ed. Graham N. Stanton (Edinburgh: T&T Clark, 1995), 119. They have little faith (8:26; 14:31; 16:8; 17:20) and he also speaks of their lack of faith (21:21) or their doubt (14:31; 28:17). They also fear as in Mt. 14:30; 17:6f; 28: 4ff. Luz also points that fear in Matthew is not connected with misunderstanding as in Mark. (*Ibid.*, 119).

[48] *Ibid.*, 120. This fits well with 15:16 and 16:9 where expressly the disciples do not yet understand. It is only in 16:12 and 17:13 that the disciples *now* understand i.e., after Jesus' exhaustive instruction. Thus, for Luz, understanding in Matthew is related to Jesus' teachings. (*Ibid.*, 121).

[49] Pointing to Matthean aim, Luz says that the disciples are portrayed in such as way as to become an example for the Matthean community. *Ibid.*, 123.

[50] *Ibid.*, 121.

[51] *Ibid.*,

[52] *Ibid.*, 123.

[53] Jack Dean Kingsbury, *Matthew as a Story* (Philadelphia: Fortress Press, 1986), 103.

[54] *Ibid.*, 111. Moreover, once having received God's kingdom with understanding, the disciples are led by it to love God with all their heart, soul and mind and neighbor as oneself (22:37) (*Ibid.*,).

[55] *Ibid.*, 112. This is in line with Jesus' assertion that the secret of the Kingdom of God has been give to the 'infants', namely the disciples.

[56] *Ibid.*, 104. This is because at this point the disciples are imperceptive and at times also resistant to the notion of servanthood as the essence of discipleship.

[57] *Ibid.*, 104. Twice in desert places Jesus expects the disciples to be cognizant of that fact that the authority with which he has endowed them (10:1) is at their disposal to feed, respectively, the five thousand and the four thousand men (14:16; 15:32-33). (*Ibid.*, 112).

[58] *Ibid.*,

[59] *Ibid.*, 103. When the disciples fail, Jesus does not leave the disciples, rather he stands ready to sustain them so that they can carry on Jesus' mission. *Ibid.*, 108.

[60] *Ibid.*, 103.

[61] Michael J. Wilkins, *Following the Master* (Grand Rapids, MI: Zondervan, 1992), 181.

[62] Similarly, at another occasion, Wilkins says that Jesus is the central figure of Matthew's gospel, p. 176. 181, Thus, most of the teaching discourses are directed towards the disciples (5:1; 10:1; 13:10, 36; 18:1; 23:1; 24:1-3), and teaching segments are often transformed into explicit discipleship-teaching pericope by inclusion of the term *disciple*. Wilkins, *Following*, 181.

[63] *Ibid.*, 180. Wilkins illustrates this from chapter 13, where Jesus initially focuses on the crowd (13:1ff). However, due to the hard heartedness, they did not understand (vv. 10-17). As a result, Jesus left the crowd to go into the privacy of the house to teach the disciples, who at the end indicated that they did understand (v. 51). Wilkins says that although the disciples were still susceptible to incomprehension and misunderstanding in his earthly ministry, Matthew emphasizes that Jesus' teaching brought them understanding and obedience. (*Ibid.*, 190). Thus, the disciples become examples of imperfect followers of Jesus who are taught and who advance in understanding and in solidarity with Jesus. (*Ibid.*, 184).

[64] *Ibid.*, 186.

[65] *Ibid.*, 181.

[66] *Ibid.*, 189.

[67] *Ibid.*, 191.

[68] *Ibid.*

[69] *Ibid.*, 315. However, this is not to say that the revolutionist view is set aside. Thus, perversity of the human 'will' explained in the moral failure of the disciples, though not directly attributed to the devil and

his agents, is not explicable in terms of a malfunction of the will. (*Ibid.*,).

[70] Riches observes a mood of deep moral seriousness and a sense of the need for a radical change of the heart is understandable (Mt. 5:8, 28; 6:21; 11:29; 12: 34; 13:15, 19; 18:35; 22:37). (*Ibid.*,)

[71] *Ibid.*,

[72] *Ibid.*, 201.

[73] *Ibid.*, 212. Explaining the role of '*will*', Riches says that Matthew adopts a restorationist view in his Gospel. However, his account of Israel's restoration is undercut by Israel's lack of understanding, its refusal to hear. What is required to understand is a deep inner reorientation to counteract the desires of the heart, which corrupts and leads people astray (Mt. 5:28; 15:18-19; 22:37). (*Ibid.*, 213).

[74] *Ibid.*, 186.

[75] *Ibid.*, 185.

[76] Leonard Doohan, *The Perennial Spirituality* (Santa Fee, New Mexico: Bear & Company, Inc. 1970), 92.

[77] *Ibid.*, 92.

[78] *Ibid.*, 93.

[79] *Ibid.*, 214.

[80] *Ibid.*, 96.

[81] *Ibid.*, 207.

[82] The faithful and observant religious leaders (Lk. 18:9-14) and the devout and morally upright young man (Lk. 18:18-30) are given examples.

[83] *Ibid.*, 210.

[84] *Ibid.*, 214.

[85] *Ibid.*,

[86] *Ibid.*, 123.

[87] *Ibid.*, 227.

[88] *Ibid.*, 123.

[89] Acts is a sequel to the Gospel of Luke and therefore, it helps to understand Luke's thought world.

[90] Brian E. Beck, *Christian Character in the Gospel of Luke* (London: Epworth, 1989), 106.

[91] *Ibid.* Beck says that though one needs to accept Conzelmann's thesis that there is a difference between the disciples' time and the Lukan community. However, unlike John (which Beck sees as an extended parable of relation between the Christ and the evangelist'

world), Luke's gospel does have a possibility of contemporary application. *Ibid.*, 105. However, Since discipleship depends on Jesus, therefore Luke intends to present lessons through the disciples' relation with Jesus, that involves more than mere imitation as, he believes that the examples only function when the power of Luke's narrative is allowed to exercise its effect directly upon the reader. *Ibid.*, 126.

92 *Ibid.*, 90.

93 *Ibid.*, 90

94 *Ibid.*, 93. Beck sees that discipleship is predominantly portrayed in the Jerusalem journey where Jesus teaches the way of God (cf. 20:21) and follows it himself. (*Ibid.*, 95, 97).

95 *Ibid.*, 95.

96 *Ibid.*, 109.

97 *Ibid.*, 114.

98 *Ibid.*, 114.

99 *Ibid.*

100 *Ibid.*, 115.

101 Jack Dean Kingsbury, *Conflict in Luke: Jesus, Authorities, Disciples* (Minneapolis: Fortress Press, 1991), 18.

102 *Ibid.*, 109. Although Jesus repeatedly tells the disciples about his passion, his predictions are nonetheless hid from them and they receive them 'without understanding' (9:44-45; 18:31-34).

103 *Ibid.*, 110.

104 They remain with Jesus in his trials (22:28-30), they continue to be obedient (22:7-13) and when Jesus announces that one who is at the table will betray (22:21-23), they all appear to be genuinely distressed. *Ibid.*, 20.

105 *Ibid.*, 126, 127.

106 *Ibid.*, 110. Based on the parable of the Sower (8:4-8), Luke asserts that true discipleship involves not only hearing the word, but holding on it and bearing fruit with endurance (8:15), in the midst of persecution, allurement of riches and perceived need to secure one's future (*Ibid.*, 114-15).

107 *Ibid.*, 120.

108 Green sees that the bottom line for Lukan discipleship is that nothing- no possessions, no relationships, no commitment, nothing – can take the place of one's relationship to Jesus and the in-breaking Kingdom of God.

109 Reminders of journey motif punctuate Luke's central section from 9:51-19:27: 9:51; 10:38; 13:22, 33; 14:25; 17:11; 18:31, 35; 19:1, 11. Through

the journey motif, Luke aims to solidify the relation between the disciples and the master and to encourage people to join him on the journey of serving God's purpose (*Ibid.*, 105). The journey motif is especially transparent in 24:13-35, where Jesus meets the two disciples on the road to Emmaus, and instructs them in the Scriptures (24:27). (*Ibid.*, 103).

[110] Joel B. Green, *Theology of Gospel of Luke.* New Testament Theology (Cambridge: Cambridge Press, 1995), 102. Longest journey is in 9:51-19:27, where Jesus teaches his disciples on the way to Jerusalem. *Ibid.*, 103.

[111] *Ibid.*, 106.

[112] *Ibid.*

[113] *Ibid.* 107. Green sees that in Luke it is the proper response to God's call of discipleship. (*Ibid.*,).

[114] Green says that the particular acute need for disciples is the need for a proper recognition of Jesus' identity and concomitant faith for his ability to provide for one's needs (8:25; 12:22-34; 16:5-6),   (*Ibid.*, 107).

[115] *Ibid.*, 103.

[116] *Ibid.*

[117] *Ibid.*, 104.

[118] *Ibid.*, 108.

[119] *Ibid.*

[120] *Ibid.*

[121] Raymond F. Collins, *These Things Have Been Written: Studies in the Fourth Gospel* (Grand Rapids, MI: William B. Eerdmans, 1990), 100.

[122] *Ibid.*

[123] *Ibid.*, 50.

[124] This phrase is not only found in the initial call narratives (1:37, 38, 41, 44), but also in the two strong sayings on discipleship (8:12; 12:26). The verb is also found in the allegory of the shepherd and his sheep (10:4, 15, 27) (*Ibid.*,).

[125] *Ibid.*, 51.

[126] *Ibid.*, 50.

[127] *Ibid.*, 127. John's use of verb 'to seek' has parallels with Heb. 'frd',' which means 'to interpret' (the Scriptures). Thus, Collins goes to argue that in John 'to seek out' the scriptures is to be led by Jesus, who not only interprets the Scriptures (6:31-33), but to whom the Scriptures points and in whom they are fulfilled. (*Ibid.*, 52).

[128] *Ibid.*, 52.

[129] *Ibid.*, 121.

[130] *Ibid.*, 50.

[131] *Ibid.*, 54.

[132] *Ibid.*, 53.

[133] *Ibid.*, 101.

[134] *Ibid.*, 54. However, true comprehension was not possible for the disciples whose faith is shown somewhat deficient due to which Judas and Thomas betray and doubt Jesus and show that they have inadequate faith. *Ibid.*, 86.

[135] *Ibid.*, 54. Regarding revelation he says that the cross is the place of supreme self-revelation. Through this Jesus reveals the earnest seeker that he abides with the Father and is now preparing a place for his disciples (*Ibid.*, 126).

[136] D. Moody Smith, *The Theology of John*. New Testament Theology (Cambridge: Cambridge University Press, 1995), 113.

[137] *Ibid.*

[138] Through the signs, which presented preliminary testimony of Jesus as God's Son and whose fuller interpretation awaited Jesus' death and exaltation. (*Ibid.*, 108-09).

[139] *Ibid.*, 114.

[140] Andreas J. Kostenberger, *The Mission of Jesus and the Disciples according to the Fourth Gospel* (Grand Rapids, MI: William B. Eerdmans, 1998), 178. The literal and symbolic meaning for the word 'follow' are used side by side in 13:36-38. (*Ibid.*,).

[141] *Ibid.*, 147. He quotes Anselm Schulz who says that that the disciples' most characteristic trait is captured by the term 'ακολυτηειν' i.e., the close relationship with his Messianic teacher...the disciples live together with their teacher (cf. 2:2, 11: 6:3, 60, 66; 11:7; 12:16; 18:2). They are those who accompany with him in his travels (cf. 2:12; 3:22; 11:7; 12:16; 18:1). They carry out various services for the master teacher (cf. 4:8, 27, 31, 33; 6: 10, 12). Finally, they witness his teaching and address their questions to him (cf. 6:60; 9:2). (*Ibid.*, 146).

[142] *Ibid.*, 145.

[143] *Ibid.*, 177. In a footnote, he shows Carson's view according to which, it is the ministry of the Holy Spirit that will enable the disciples to understand fully Jesus' words and works.

[144] *Ibid.*, 173.

[145] Cornelis Bennema, *The Power of Saving Wisdom: An Investigation of Spirit and Wisdom in Relation to the Soteriology of the Fourth Gospel* (Tübingen: Mohr Siebeck, 2002),127.

[146] *Ibid.*, 132.

[147] *Ibid.*, 139.

[148] *Ibid.*, italics added. Bennema sees that the knowledge available to a believer makes it possible to know the will of the Father and the Son and therefore, to demonstrate discipleship (cf. 7:17; 8:31-32; 10:4; 13:17; 15:15; 15:27-16:4; cf. Jesus' obedience because he knows the Father 8:55; cf. 2:24-25; 13:1; 18:4). (*Ibid.*, 129).

[149] *Ibid.*, 121.

[150] *Ibid.*, 132.

[151] Jesus calls people to follow him (1:43; 12:26; 21:19, 22), not all continuously follow him (either because their motives were wrong or because they find Jesus' teaching offensive and too demanding), and therefore they fail to remain in a saving relationship with Jesus (*Ibid.*, 141). Thus, remaining is saving relationship with Jesus is possible, when one continues to accept (by understanding and obeying) Jesus' commands (that are at times, offensive and too demanding) (*Ibid.*,).

[152] Bennema explains that continuation of believers' friendship (fellowship) with the Father depends upon the believer's obedience to Jesus (15:14), as well as her/his continuous knowing and understanding of the Father and Son. (*Ibid.*, 139, 129). Author emphasizes the role of the cognitive aspect of mind, when he says that to sustain one's salvation, one needs to cognitively perceive the mediated truth (*Ibid.*, 121). Thus, remaining in salvation and thereby in discipleship, by implication, depends both upon understanding and in obeying Jesus' words.

[153] *Ibid.*, 140.

[154] *Ibid.*, 119.

[155] *Ibid.*, 120.

[156] *Ibid.*, 121.

[157] Therefore, author suggests that to hear means to understand the life giving words of Jesus and therefore, to recognize his true identity. Similarly, to see Jesus and in him the Father is to identify and understand their work, and relationship. This leads to life (6:40; 7:31; 11:45; 12:9-11), (*Ibid.*,) At other occasion, author clarifies that though belief based on signs can be adequate, in John true saving belief should still be based on true understanding, and cannot bypass cognitive perception (10:38; 14:11). (*Ibid.*, 146).

[158] *Ibid.*, 125. However, Bennema also points out that not all cognitive perception necessarily leads one to salvation, which is clear from the initial life of Nicodemus, (*Ibid.*, 127). In addition, he sees that the Holy

Spirit also plays an important role in revealing the truth about Jesus. (*Ibid.*, 129).

[159] One of the key proponent of this view is G. Strecker (Ulrich Luz, "The Disciples in the Gospel according to Matthew," in *The Interpretation of Matthew,* ed. Graham Stanton (Edinburgh: T&T Clark, 1995), 115.

[160] This approach has been taken by Hummel (Ulrich Luz, "The Disciples in the Gospel according to Matthew," in *The Interpretation of Matthew,* ed. Graham Stanton (Edinburgh: T&T Clark, 1995), 115.

[161] I share this stance with scholars like Ulrich Luz (R. T. France, *Matthew: Evangelist and Teacher* (Grand Rapids, Michigan: Academie Books (Zondervan), 1989), 199; Wilkins (M. J. Wilkins, "Discipleship," in *DJG,* eds. Joel B. Green and Scot McKnight (Leicester: IVP, 1992), 182; Beck (Brian E. Beck, *Christian Character in the Gospel of Luke* (London: Epworth, 1989), 106; Tuckett (C.M. Tuckett, "Synoptic Problem," in *ABD,* ed. David Noel Freedman, vol. 6 (New York: Doubleday, 1992), 336, along with many others.

CHAPTER 1

The Role of the Mind in Markan Discipleship

Lord and Savior, true and kind, be the master of my mind; Bless and guide and strengthen still all my powers of thought and will. While I ply the scholars' task, Jesus Christ be near, I ask; Help the memory, clear the brain, knowledge still to seek and gain.

—Bishop H. G. C. Moule[1]

Introduction

Markan priority assumes that the Gospel of Mark is the earliest written canonical account of Jesus' life and ministry. Therefore, we shall study this Gospel first. This chapter aims to explore the role of cognitive function of the mind or, in other words, the role of "understanding" in Markan discipleship. To this end, we begin with understanding the nature of Mark's Gospel, as this would aid us in exploring the Markan epistemological framework. After doing this, we will examine the theme of incomprehension, which stands as one of the most dominant themes in the Gospel of Mark.[2] Based on the above study, we will uncover the role of understanding in discipleship as Mark presents it through his Gospel.

Nature of the Markan Community

Mark explains several Jewish customs, Aramaic terms and phrases (e.g. 7: 34; 15:34), which suggests that the original audience of

Mark's Gospel lived outside Palestine. Pointing to the geographical location, Balabanski suggests that the community lived in Syria.[3] However, Witherington, based upon references to persecution, ascribes Rome as the native place for the Markan community.[4] Besides the question of location, the question about the context of writing stands as of greater import for our discussion. There is a fair consensus regarding the context and occasion for Mark's Gospel. Peterson in line with Balabanski views that the recipients were an "apocalyptic community",[5] who hoped that the eschatological climax would come in the near future (Mk. 13:21-23; Lk. 19:11; Acts 1:6).[6] To this, Witherington adds that during this time, the community saw many false prophets and fanatics who claimed that the end is already come.[7]

Based on several references to suffering (4:17; 8:34-9:1; 13:9, 11-13), Marcus suggests that the community was undergoing severe persecution.[8] Rikki Watts assumes—based on the editorial comments at the opening of the Gospel in 1:1-3 and frequent OT citations (7:6-7, 10, 10:5, 19f)—that the community had a strong Jewish background.[9]

Regarding the purpose of Mark, Shiner says there is little doubt that among other things, Mark had intended to reinforce his audience's conviction that Jesus is the Messiah, the Son of God, and to teach them their own responsibilities as Jesus' followers.[10] Based on the above observations, we contend that the recipients were an apocalyptic community (that eagerly awaited the Lord's glorious return on the clouds), with a Jewish connection[11] and one that was undergoing severe persecution because of their faith.

Markan Discipleship: A Portrait

Many scholars[12] have suggested that the main teaching on discipleship is found in Mk. 8:27-10:45. Telford observes that the Markan narrative technique of placing the central section on discipleship between the healing of two blind men in 8:22-26 and 10:46-52, suggests that discipleship is like the healing of the blind by Jesus.[13] Mark seems to present discipleship as the life of those who have committed themselves to Jesus (3:7; 6:1; 8:27; 10:32; 11:20;

13:1; 14:32); a life that is characterised as a process of gaining understanding like the healing of the blind man in stages in 8:22-26.[14]

Shiner comments on Markan discipleship and observes that the goal of a follower of Jesus is the kingdom of God and to be included among the elect in the end (13:27), rather than learning a system of thought or a way of life. He argues that Mark emphasises the necessity for followers to abandon all else in their devotion to Jesus.[15] Watts shows how Mark presents discipleship in terms of Isaiahnic New Exodus (INE).[16] So, Mark seems to suggest that following Jesus is to follow God in his plan of salvation predicated on the death and resurrection of Jesus.

Similarly, commenting upon the essence of discipleship, Witherington sees it as possible only when one denies herself or himself (8:34) and relies on Jesus through faith.[17] Thus, Mark sees discipleship as a life of total commitment to Jesus as one's Lord and Master and a life of following continuously, irrespective of the failures, so that ultimately one will be found among the elect ones of God's community.

Nature of Mark's Gospel

Mark's opening editorial in 1:1-3 indicates that Mark writes with a strong Old Testament presupposition about the promised eschatological visitation of Yahweh to fulfill the promised INE.[18] Mark 10:42 has unusual Greek construction ("those who are thought to rule over the Gentiles"); it does not simply say "those who are rulers of the Gentiles" in Matthew and Luke. Based on this, Marcus argues for the apocalyptic nature of the Gospel.[19] This view sees that those who are commonly thought to be rulers are not the real rulers as, behind them, stand the real rulers, God and Satan, each with a host of servants.[20] In addition, Horsley points to the cosmic nature of the Gospel when he says that Satan and the unclean spirits play a key role in the Markan drama. And he sees that early in the Gospel, they are "bound" implying that they are already defeated.[21] Thus, Mark's Gospel presents the life and ministry of Jesus in the light of God's activity to effect salvation to all who believe.[22]

Similarly, Geddert argues for the apocalyptic nature of the Gospel and shows as evidence the presence of inseparable apocalyptic promises attached to calls for discipleship (8:31-9:1; 10:17-31).[23] Marcus says that Mark's apocalyptic nature is clear in Jesus' inaugural sermon ('time is fulfilled', 1:14-15) and when Jesus says that some will not taste death before the Kingdom of God comes to power (9:1).[24]

Thus, we contend that Mark presents discipleship from an apocalyptic view of reality, implying that a disciple ought to interpret the present earthly events in the light of the invading Kingdom of God, initiated in the coming of Jesus Christ. In this way, Mark's Gospel stands as a window to understanding the real significance of everyday earthly events.

Markan Epistemology

This section aims to outline the framework of Markan epistemology. Though Mark has not intended to present a detailed epistemology in clearly defined philosophical categories, he does operate under an epistemological framework, which is important to explore as we seek to explore the role of understanding in Markan discipleship. Since Mark's Gospel is written from an apocalyptic point of view, holding that the revelation of the heavenly events provides a key to understanding earthly events, it implies that Mark's epistemology is coloured by his apocalyptic world view. In other words, Markan epistemology can be explained in terms of his apocalyptic understanding. This means that the theme of the "disciples' incomprehension" (which stands as an index of Mark's epistemological understanding) can be explained in the light of Mark's apocalyptic view. In view of the obvious divine intent present in Mark 4:10-12, Marcus rightly explains that it stands as one of the most important texts that shed light on the Markan apocalyptic view.[25] We will now take a look at this subject and other related texts.

Insiders and *Outsiders*

Mark 4:11-12 is considered as one of the key texts to unlock the Markan epistemological framework.[26] Through this Mark aims to show that the knowledge of the secret of the kingdom of God[27] (which is bound up in the person of Jesus) is a gift and is not based on human intellect. Marcus makes this point when he observes Mark's uses of the verb "has been given" in Mk. 4:11.[28] This premise assumes that humanity is confounded with an epistemic darkness, from which it cannot come out on its own. At this point, Jesus' teachings (the parables in Mark) play a significant role by becoming a window to a deeper reality about Jesus. Telford sees Jesus' parables as conveying a cryptic message about Jesus as "the Son of God."[29]

However, not all come to perceive this reality. Regarding the parable of the sower, Marcus sees that since there is no indication of change in soil type, only those who have been chosen by God to know His secret will be able to understand the hidden truth about Jesus' words.[30] He thus concludes that God stands behind the eye-opening of some (insiders) and blinding of others (outsiders) mediated by the powers of darkness (Mk.4:15).[31] However, Riches counter argues and views the above arguments by Marcus to be at odds with Mk. 4:10-12, where it is the parables that are the means whereby God hardens people's responses to his revelation.[32] Riches sees that such a reading also explains well the three-fold injunction to hear at Mark 4:3, 9, 23.[33] Regarding this, Marcus says that though autonomy is granted to human beings in matters of understanding, it is severely limited.[34] As this explanation is too vague, this not only weakens Marcus' view, but also stands favoring Riches' view regarding the human need to make efforts to hear and understand and thereby to make an appropriate response.

Contrary to Marcus' position, Mark 6:52 further gives indication that God is not deliberately involved in blinding the "outsiders." This passage explains the disciples as those "whose hearts were hardened", thereby becoming exactly like the "outsiders" mentioned in 4:12. Shiner along with Marcus[35] sees this hardening as analogous to the hardening of Pharaoh in Exodus. However, Shiner moves away from Marcus' view in his subsequent description of the disciples' hardening in Mk. 6:52. Shiner argues that at Mark 6:52, Mark faced the problem of making plausible the disciples' hardness in failing to understand.[36] Shiner says that the only possible way Mark could maintain both the Son of God's omnipotence and his seeming inability to convince the disciples of his divine identity was to ascribe their incomprehension to God.[37] Thus, Shiner does not see a deliberate hand of God in blinding the "outsiders."

Leander E. Keck takes a similar stand when it argues that 4:12 should not be seen as a deliberate attempt to exclude people from hearing the message, because Jesus would not endorse the policy of cutting off access of forgiveness, as he came for this very reason (Mk. 1:15; 2:5, 10, 17).[38] Lane also subscribes to this view when he says that it is unbelief that ultimately makes Jesus' words a riddle.[39] The above argument points to the fact that God is not deliberately involved in the blinding of outsiders.[40] The above discussion also indicates that humans fall into the "outsiders" category because of their own negligence and unbelief. It is for such a group of people that Jesus' parabolic teachings become an agent of concealment rather than revelation.

Regarding the central issue behind incomprehension, Watts says, "It is not whether one sees (for in one sense all human observers involved are blind and laboring under misconceptions of some sort), instead the issue is whether or not one is willing to let go of conventional wisdom, to follow and 'be found and around' Jesus and so know the mystery of the kingdom of God made revealed in Jesus."[41] Based upon Mk. 6:1-6, Barton says there is a conflict between conventional and revealed wisdom and only those who lean on Jesus by faith will receive the "mystery" of the kingdom of God.[42] In the end, the parables divide humanity into two categories: those who understand Jesus' parables "insiders" and those who do not understand them "outsiders."

Interestingly, even though the "insiders" received Jesus' private teaching, they frequently failed to understand the significance of Jesus' presence and the meaning of his teachings. Based on 4:22-23, Marcus relates their incomprehension to their temporal situation, being in the penultimate age during which complete or adequate understanding about Jesus was not possible for the "insiders."[43] At the turning point of the ages, the Cross reveals the previously hidden secrets to all humankind.[44] This is plausible as for Mark the Cross is the most important point and he sees it as an apocalyptic event. However, Mark does not seem to look at the event of the Cross as a reason for the disciples' lack of understanding and misunderstandings before it. This is clear as Jesus expresses his frustration when the disciples do not understand (Mk. 4:13; 6:52; 8:17-21). Thus, we contend that an adequate understanding was possible to make a saving belief response before the Cross, which is why the disciples had become "insiders" in contrast to the "outsiders."

The evidence of understanding after the Cross is found in Mk.16:8. Regarding this, Marcus says that a lack of understanding continues to affect the disciples even after the Cross. He attributes their bewilderment to the continuing activity of the powers of darkness.[45] Since the disciples remain susceptible to incomprehension even after the Cross, it suggests that Mark was pointing to the serious results of not understanding the truth about Jesus' identity and his teachings and, therefore, sought to exhort his readers to apply their minds to (to hear) understand Jesus and his instruction aright. This points to the importance of the role of the cognitive function of the mind in discipleship.

The encouraging fact is that Jesus patiently continues to teach the disciples ("insiders") even as they consistently followed him. This shows that the position of disciples as "insiders" is ultimately not based upon their superior character or wisdom but upon God's act of grace. Marcus says (based upon the story of Bartimaeus in Mk. 10:46-52) that faith and following Jesus mark the entry and condition of remaining within the scope of revelation.[46] This points to the ongoing nature of salvation.

Myers points to the need for a believing response in order to understand Jesus and his instruction. Commenting upon Jesus' response to the scribe in Mk.12:34, Myers says that it implies that mere intellectual assent to Jesus' teachings without accepting him as one's Lord is insufficient to become a part of God's community.[47] Rowland reminds us that the Gospel writers wrote with a conviction that the ancient quest for wisdom finds its true goal in Jesus, the Christ.[48] In other words, if one rejects Jesus, it is like rejecting true wisdom and ending up as an "outsider." Thus, we believe that Mark highlights that accepting Jesus and his teachings opens up a person to understand the otherwise hidden cosmic reality. In other words, knowing Jesus and his teachings makes it possible not only to become an "insider",[49] but also to understand the real meaning behind everyday events. To put it differently, accepting Jesus not only makes one a member of God's elect community, but also enables a disciple to understand Jesus and his teachings.

Moreover, Mark seems to argue that for an "insider" Jesus' instructions become an epistemic window that enables her or him to understand the true significance of earthly events. Shiner makes a similar point when he says that in Mark the divine reality, which remains hidden, overlaps the mundane world through the person of Jesus.[50] This reality is revealed to the "insiders", who simply stick with Jesus. Jesus defines them as those who do the will of the Father (3:35). Thus, Mark aims to show that to remain within the scope of God's revelation, one is called to continually grow in understanding by applying one's cognitive abilities to understand Jesus and his instruction, which is possible as a disciple walks in obedience to the given revelation. Thus, obedience facilitates understanding and understanding leads to further obedience in the path of discipleship.

The Cross: Climax of Jesus' Self-expression

Mark sees the Cross as one of the most important points of his narrative. Regarding the Cross, Green says that for Mark Jesus' death is the moment of divine revelation—that place and time where Jesus' identity could be fully appreciated.[51] This is also clear as he relates the crucifixion to apocalyptic events; the complete darkness at noon, symbolising the darkness of the "day of the Lord" and cry of dereliction and sorrow as Jesus was about to identify fully with human estrangement from God (Mk. 15:33-34). Similarly, J. Schreiber has argued that crucifixion contains apocalyptic elements: the cosmic darkness (15:38), noting the hourly schedule as events occurred (15:25, 33, 34a) and the primordial silence, which is broken by Jesus' cry (15:37).[52] Like Marcus,[53] Telford sees that Mark 4:21-22 points to the Cross. Thus, we find that Mark sees the Cross as an eschatological event that culminates in the plan of Jesus' coming to the earth (Mk. 10:45) and, therefore, stands as the highest point of his self-disclosure.

However, even the crucifixion does not guarantee that one will come to a knowledge about Jesus without misunderstanding. Marcus points out that though the disciples are promised a vision of Jesus in Mk.16:7, there are still those among them who will look and look but never understand. Pointing to Mk.13:26, Marcus goes on to say that it is only at the parousia that the veil will be lifted completely.[54] Thus, while the Cross marks a new eschatological era of a fuller revelation, Mark suggests that the paradoxical hiddenness of God's revelation continues to be at work among the believers (seen in the negative portrait of the women in Mk. 16:8), and by implication also among the unbelievers.

Theme of Disciples' Incomprehension
The theme of incomprehension, as already noted before, is one of the dominant themes in Mark's Gospel. While the disciples are portrayed in a positive light in the first three chapters (1:18; 2:14; 2: 23f; 3:13f), they begin to show signs of incomprehension from chapter four onwards. The discipleship teachings are found in 8:27-10:52, where the disciples continued to misunderstand Jesus' evaluative point of view. Thus, even when Peter (and by implication the remaining disciples[55]) confesses Jesus as 'the Christ' in 8: 27, the disciples continue to misunderstand and show signs of lack of comprehension (8:32; 9:6 cf. 14:50; 9:10; 9:38f; 10:26; 10:35-

37). Ultimately, it leads them to desert Jesus at the time of his arrest (Mk. 14:50).

However, Mark's primary focus on the disciples' incomprehension (regarding Jesus' identity as "Son of God") falls in the preceding section (4:1-8:26), which stands as a unified whole. It ultimately leads Jesus to rebuke the disciples (8:17-18) in a language used to characterise "those outside" in Mark 4:11-12.[56] Shiner sees the episode 4:1-8:26 as containing several incidents concerning the disciples' incomprehension and which are interrelated by verbal and thematic similarities.[57] This suggests that the listener should interpret all the specific episodes as having the same unified theme.[58] Thus, we shall be primarily focusing on section 4:1-8:26.

Purpose of Disciples' Incomprehension

Regarding the disciples' incomprehension, Marcus suggests that the spirit of darkness was influencing even them, so that frequently they failed to understand the significance of Jesus' words and deeds. Based upon Mark 4:13-20; 7:17f; 9:28-9; 10:10-12l; 13:3ff, Telford sees two functions of the disciples' portrait as foils for Jesus. Firstly, the disciples, by appearing frail, confused, afraid and human, make Jesus with all his authority and dignity as the Lord of the Church stand in contrast to them. Secondly, by repeatedly misunderstanding him, they offer Jesus an opportunity to teach on the true nature of his person and mission, as well as unavoidable discipleship springing from it.[59]

Marcus says that the disciples dramatised the Markan audiences' frustration at trying to make sense of Jesus' identity. This shared frustration serves both to tie the audience to the disciples and to highlight the transcendence of Jesus.[60] Throughout Mark's Gospel, the purpose behind the incomprehension of the disciples is to make a rhetorical point about Jesus' identity (and discipleship).[61] Mark aims to illustrate through the disciples' example the challenge of understanding Jesus as the Lord and of continually following him with a curious mind.

Thematic Study of the Disciples' Incomprehension in Mark

As mentioned earlier, the section within Mk. 4:1-8:26 encloses the theme of incomprehension, which is spread throughout the constituting episodes. This section is primarily made up of miracles and parables, which serve to reveal (or conceal) Jesus' identity. Regarding the miracles and parables, Shiner sees an analogy between them, as he says that Mark uses Isaiahnic language in 8:17-18.[62] Similarly, Watts sees a connection between the parable chapter(s) and miracles (4:35-5:43) and says that they both raise the question of Jesus' identity and the significance of his actions.[63] Therefore, we will trace the theme of the disciples' incomprehension in this section as a whole.

The first instance of the disciples' incomprehension in Mark 4:13 is significant, as we argued before, since it establishes that the disciples' understanding (though imperfect) of the secret of kingdom of God as God's gracious gift is not based upon their human intellect. Regarding the nature of Jesus' teaching, Shiner points out that the most important aspect of Jesus' teaching is not the content, but the nature of his teaching–through parables.[64] He sees the parable of the sower as forming a chiasm, whose centre point is 4:11-12. This suggests that Jesus' teaching, which is inextricably bound to his identity, is not evident on the surface, but is rather hidden inside the symbols of the parable. It is precisely this nature of the parables, which results in the division of people into "insiders" or "outsiders." The disciples' incomprehension is clear from Mk. 4:13, which Shiner sees as a Markan technique to reinforce the listener's awareness of the difficulty of understanding.[65]

The other important pericope is Mark 7:14-23 that has verbal similarities with 4:1-20.[66] This indicates that this section could be interpreted along the same line as 4:1-20.[67] In each case, Jesus expected the disciples to understand, but while he expressed his disappointment, he immediately provides an explanation. Thus, as Shiner suggests, this section again underscores the general difficulty in understanding.[68] We now turn to the consideration of the miracles of Jesus.

We notice that right from the first miracle in Mark 4:35f (first of the three boat scenes in 4:35f), Mark's persistent question about Jesus' identity finds its first expression. Interestingly, Watts points out that the disciples' incomprehension is also found in the intervening and final boat scenes (6:45-52; 8:14-21).[69] The relationship between the boat scenes and the feeding miracle(s) (in 6:30-44 and 8:1-13) is clear as Mark mentions about the loaves both in the second (6:52) and final boat scenes (8:16). Through the event of Jesus stilling the storm, Mark aims to present Jesus not only as the Messiah, but also (as Watts suggests) as the actual presence of Yahweh himself, Jesus exercising authority only associated with Yahweh himself.[70] However, this seemed to be too esoteric for the disciples to grasp and, therefore, they responded in fear and amazement. The feeding miracle (6:30-44), as Watts rightly suggests, should have caused the disciples to see Jesus as Israel's servant Messiah.[71] However, as Watts says, since they did not even understand the significance of the feeding miracle, they also failed to understand the significance of the following boat scene explained in 6:52, it being a miracle of a higher order.[72]

Jesus' identity and significance is the primary emphasis of the text up to 8:14-21. It is also clear through the Markan construction in placing the healing of the blind in stages (8:22-26) and the story of Peter's confession (8:27f) immediately after his warning (about the leaven of the Pharisees), which seems to interpret the final boat section.[73] Regarding the leaven of the Pharisees, Shiner says that by pointing to the Pharisees and Herod, Mark aims to confront the listener with a demand to interpret the entire section from 4:1ff onwards and, by linking the bread and sea miracles with Peter's confession, to supply an answer about the truth of Jesus' identity, which Jesus did not give in the final boat scene in 8:14-21.[74] Regarding the leaven of Herod and the Pharisees, Shiner sees it as referring to human wisdom. The same is evident in Jesus' rebuke of Peter in 8:33.[75] Moreover, as Shiner has suggested, Peter's consorting with Satan in his objection to the passion communicated very clearly to the Markan audience the serious need for a proper understanding.[76] Through this theme, Mark aimed to portray

Christ as the "Son of God", who would lead his people into a life of discipleship, whose perfect model is found in the life and teachings of Jesus himself.

Command to Love God with the Mind

The disciples' failures, particularly related to incomprehension, provided for them a challenge: How to understand the true nature and mission of Jesus and, as a corollary; what was theirs? One of the interesting points is Mark's reference to the question of the Pharisees concerning the greatest commandment in the Bible (12:30). Regarding the relevance of this question, Evans says that it was to ascertain the most important commandment that would provide the surest hope of securing one's place within God's community.[77] In response to the question, Jesus quotes the Jewish 'Shema' mentioned in Deuteronomy 6:5. Interestingly, as Jesus quotes it, he adds to the Deuteronomic passage, the word "mind" (Gk. Διανοια) to the list of three (καρδια [heart]; ψυχη [soul]; ἰσχυρος [strength]), when heart (καρδια) already includes the notion of "mind."[78] Let us briefly look at the meaning of heart (καρδια) and mind (διανοια) to explore the possible reason behind the Markan addition of δαινοια.

Καρδια or Heart

In the LXX, καρδια usually translates the Heb. לב, which denotes the seat of mental and spiritual capacities. It was the seat of rational functions and of accepting divine teachings (Pr. 7:3).[79] Thus, it was equivalent to "mind." In Hellenistic Judaism, as in OT tradition, it meant the centre of the human person and the source of his moral and spiritual life.[80] However, among the Greeks, καρδια was used literally to represent an organ in the chest.[81]

Διανοια Mind

In extra-biblical literature, this term was used in a variety of ways and as an alternative to νους[82,83] and it distinguished humans from beasts.[84] In the LXX, διανοια was used to translate "heart" and, therefore, stood equivalent to καρδια,[85] which was seen as the centre of one's inner life.

Regarding the terms used in Mk. 12:30, Evans says that they are decidedly not synonymous, and Mark may have added διανοια to emphasise the need to love God with the totality of our being.[86] The view that Mark does not aim to portray a rigid concept of personhood, but to highlight a totality of personhood in devotion to God is also held by Bandstra and Stuart.[87] Similarly, Gould says that there is no attempt to classify human personhood, but there is an attempt to express, in a strong way, the whole being.[88] Moreover, as we have seen, the Markan community was Greek-speaking and lived in the Gentile territory of Syria.[89] The fact that Mark aimed to add διανοια to the list of three in "Shema" is plausible for two reasons: Firstly, since καρδια meant a physical organ in the Greek thought world, Mark removes the possibility of limiting the meaning of the LXX rendering of καρδια (Heb. βλε) to just a physical organ. Secondly, Mark aimed to emphasise the vital need for understanding Jesus and his mission. Thus, through the addition of διανοια Mark exhorts the disciples to apply their minds to knowing and following Jesus consistently, and he warns them against complacency and falling away.

Markan Epistemology and Community

As noted earlier, the Markan community was undergoing severe persecution. Confronted by the hostile world, the community would have been asking among themselves as to why people were not recognising who Jesus was. Mark 4:11-12, as Marcus suggests, must have provided an answer, according to which the world outside was mysteriously blinded by the forces of darkness.[90] Thus, Mark's Gospel would have given a paradigm to understand the day-to-day events in the light of something profound going on in the spirit world. Moreover, now since Jesus has already overpowered the powers of darkness (3:23-29), they can rest assured that ultimately, God will vindicate his elect and in the light of which, facing the present sufferings is not to be considered too weighty to bear.

Conclusion

We examined Mark's epistemology and his theology behind the theme of incomprehension. Mark presents Jesus as God's promised Son through whom, He reveals himself to the world. This truth is revealed to the disciples, which is God's gift of grace to the disciples (or insiders). However, in spite of Jesus' continual explanations to them, the disciples failed frequently to understand Jesus and his evaluative point of view. Through this, Mark aimed to show the great difficulty involved in understanding the true nature of Jesus and his mission. The knowledge of this truth in a growing manner is essential for growing in discipleship. This knowledge comes by making an adequate believing response to Jesus and obeying what is revealed.

Knowledge of Jesus and his purpose also provides the disciples with a window to understanding their present circumstances. It is because of a fuller understanding of Jesus' identity that now the disciples can face persecution and do not think it foolish to embrace a life of Cross bearing. This is because the present world is not the end, but only a precursor to the eternal age, which Jesus has already inaugurated by his death and resurrection.

End Notes

[1] Quoted in J. P. Moreland, *Love Your God with All Your Mind: The Role of Reason in the Life of the Soul* (Colorado, Colorado Springs: Navpress, 1997), 155.

[2] William R. Telford, *The Theology of the Gospel of Mark*, NTT (Cambridge: Cambridge University Press, 1999), 154 and 218; John Hargreaves, *A Guide to St. Mark's Gospel* (Cambridge: Cambridge University Press, 1965), 191.

[3] Vicky Balabanski, *Eschatology in the Making* (Oakleigh, Melbourne: Cambridge University Press, 1997), 62.

[4] Ben Witherington III, *The Rhetoric of Mark: A Socio Rhetorical Commentary* (Grand Rapids, Michigan: Eerdmans, 2000), 27.

[5] Dwight N. Peterson , *The Origins of Mark: The Markan Community in Current Debate* (Netherlands, Leiden: Brill, 2000), 63.

[6] D. C. Allison, "Apocalypse," in *DJG*, eds. Joel B. Green and Scot McKnight (Leicester: IVP, 1992), 19.

THE ROLE OF THE MIND IN MARKAN DISCIPLESHIP   45

[7] Witherington, *Rhetoric*, 337.

[8] Joel Marcus, "Mark 4:10-12 and Marcan Epistemology"*JBL* 103 No 4 (1984): 572.

[9] Rikki E. Watts, *Isaiah's New Exodus in Mark*, (Grand Rapids, Michigan: Eerdmans, 1997), 120.

[10] Whitney P. Shiner, *Follow Me! Disciples in Mark*, SBL Diss. Ser., 145 (Atlanta, Georgia: Scholars Press, 1995), 6.

[11] However, I do not assume that the community did not have Gentile Christians from Hellenistic background.

[12] John G. Cook, *The Structure and the Persuasive Power of Mark: A Linguistic Approach*. SBL Sem. Ser. (Atlanta, Georgia: Scholars Press, 1995), 162; Michael J. Wilkins, *Following the Master* (Grand Rapids, Michigan: Zondervan, 1992), 199;   John K. Riches, *Conflicting Mythologies*, SNTW (Edinburgh: T&T Clark, 2000), 73; Shiner, *Follow Me!*, 278; Telford, *The Theology*, 51- 52 and 105.

[13] Telford, *The Theology*, 100.

[14] Riches, *Conflicting*, 72; Rhoads, *Mark*, 126.

[15] Shiner, *Follow Me!*, 253.

[16] Watts, *Isaiah's*, 223.

[17] Witherington, *Rhetoric*, 434.

[18] Watts contends that Mark's threefold structure, viz. (i) Jesus' powerful ministry in Galilee and beyond, (ii) his leading his 'blind' disciples along with 'Way', and (iii) arrival in Jerusalem, echoes the Isaianic New Exodus schema, where Yahweh as Warrior and Healer delivers his people from bondage, leads the 'blind' along the NE way of deliverance, and arrives in Jerusalem. (Watts, *Isaiah's*, 5.)

[19] Marcus, "Mark 4:10-12", 557.

[20] *Ibid.*, 558.

[21] Richard Horsley, "Wisdom and Apocalypticism in Mark," in *In Search of Wisdom: Essays in Memory of John G. Gammie*, eds. Leo G. Perdue, et al. (Louisville, Kentucky: Westminster, 1993), 234.

[22] Marcus, "Mark 4:10-12", 557.

[23] *Ibid.*, 25.

[24] Joel Marcus, *Mark1-8*, ABC (New York: Doubleday, 1999), 71.

[25] Marcus, "Mark 4:10-12", 557.

[26] *Ibid.*

[27] Regarding the meaning of the secret of the Kingdom of God, Telford sees it as the mystery bound up and revealed in Jesus Christ (Telford, *Theology*, 156). Lane holds a similar position when he says that in Mk. 4:11, Jesus was not thinking of the kingdom of God in any

abstract sense whether as a future or a present reality, but of the kingdom embodied in his own person. (William L. Lane, *The Gospel of Mark*, in New International Commentary on New Testament (Grand Rapids, Michigan: Eerdmans, 1974), 157.

[28] Marcus, "Mark 4:10-12", 558.

[29] Telford, *Theology*, 156. He sees this as an outcome of the shift in emphasis in the parables (as in the title 'Son of Man') from apocalyptic eschatology to Christology and soteriology.

[30] Marcus, "Mark 4:10-12", 566. Marcus also quotes Jeremias who sees that verbs 'δέδοται', 'γίνεται' and 'ἀπῄετηε' in 4:11-12 as circumlocutions of divine activity, which imply that God stands behind the eye-opening of 'insiders' and blinding of 'outsiders' described in Mark, 561.

[31] Marcus, "Mark 4:10-12", 561.

[32] Riches, *Conflicting*, 155.

[33] *Ibid.*, 155.

[34] *Ibid.*, 562.

[35] Marcus, *Mark 1-8*, 428.

[36] Shiner, *Follow Me!*, 251.

[37] *Ibid.*

[38] Leander E. Keck, ed., *The New Interpreter's Bible*, vol. 8 (Nashville: Abingdon, 1995), 572.

[39] William Lane, *Gospel of Mark*, The New Commentary of the New Testament (London: Morgan Marshall and Scott Company, 1974), 158.

[40] Moreover, the attacks of Satan (v. 15), tribulations (v. 17) and worries of life, the deceitfulness of wealth and the desires for other things (v. 19) are experiences that are not applicable to a fixed predetermined number of people, but to the entire human race.

[41] Watts, *Isaiah's*, 206. Watts also points to the three main opinions among scholars about the disciples' incomprehension: the first group (Meye; Budesheim; Schmahl and Stock) suggest that they are guarantors of the tradition. The second group (Tyson; Weeden; Kuby; Kelber) sees them proxies for Mark's opponents and as such are little better than heretical reprobates. However, the third group to which Watts belongs (Reploh, Lehrer; Focant; Hawkin; Best; Malbon) assert that the disciples' successes and failures both serve to encourage Mark's audience. *Ibid.*, 222.

[42] Stephen C. Barton, "Gospel Wisdom," in *Where Shall Wisdom be Found*, ed. Stephen C. Barton (Edinburgh: T&T Clark, 1999), 101.

[43] Marcus, "Mark 4:10-12", 568.

[44] *Ibid.,* 570.

[45] *Ibid.,* 572.

[46] *Ibid.*

[47] Chad Myers, *Binding the Strong Man: A Political Reading of Mark's Story of Jesus* (Maryknoll, NY: Orbis Books, 1997), 318.

[48] Christopher Rowland, "Sweet Science Reigns: Divine and Human Wisdom in the Apocalyptic Tradition," in *Where Shall Wisdom be Found,* ed. Stephen C. Barton (Edinburgh: T&T Clark, 1999), 94.

[49] Which is the ultimate behind the writing of the Gospel.

[50] Shiner, *Follow Me!,* 241.

[51] Joel B. Green, "Death of Jesus," in *DJG,* eds. Joel B. Green and Scott McKnight (Leicester: IVP, 1992), 158. Green makes such an assertion as he argues that Jesus' death functions as the center of God's redemptive plan that comes to light in two Markan texts:10:45 and 14:24, where Jesus' death is interpreted as salvific. (*Ibid.,*)

[52] Marcus, *Mark1-8,* 9.

[53] Marcus, "Mark 4:10-12", 573.

[54] Marcus, "Mark 4:10-12", 572.

[55] This is because, it appears that Peter was the disciples' representative based on following evidences: 8:29-30; 9: 6; 14:29. He is also one among the inner circle (14:33).

[56] There is only one exception to this in 6:7-13, 30. Shiner sees this section as very important as it is a framing technique that frames the ministry of the disciples and story of John the Baptist. Shiner (Shiner, *Follow Me!,* 250.) along with Telford (Telford , *Theology,* 133) asserts that in Mark the episodes within a frame are interconnected. Thus, through the section 6:7-30, Mark associates the disciples' successful ministry with the death of John the Baptist, thereby suggesting that the disciples like John may be required to give up their lives.

[57] Shiner shows that unity of the section 4:1-8:26 has been argued by various scholars like: Weeden, Kelber, Madelein Boucher and Frank J. Matera. (Shiner, *Follow Me!,* 199).

[58] *Ibid.,* 199.

[59] Telford, *Theology,* 132. He sees some similarities in the disciples and the anticipated readers, who by the disciples' incomprehension are invited to identify and failure, as prototypical Christians, and so, by such identification, be led to both self-criticism and comfort.

[60] Marcus, "Mark 4:10-12", 512-13.

[61] Shiner, *Follow Me!,* 30.

[62] Shiner, *Follow Me!,* 199.

[63] Watts, *Isaiah's*, 228.

[64] Shiner, *Follow Me!*, 202. This fact is evident as Jesus' parabolic teaching is mentioned at the beginning and the end of the discourse (4:2; 4: 33-34).

[65] *Ibid.*, 206.

[66] Shiner shows a detailed comparative outline of both sections in the following way: 4:3a par. 7:14; 4:3b-8 par. 7:15; 4:9 par. 7:16; 4:10 par. 4:17; 4:10 par. 7:17; 4:11-12 explanation of speaking in parables; 4:13 par. 7: 18a; 4:14-20 par. 7: 18b-23. Shiner, *Follow Me!*, 210-11.

[67] *Ibid.*, 209.

[68] *Ibid.*

[69] Watts, *Isaiah's*, 229.

[70] *Ibid.*, 231.

[71] *Ibid.*, 232.

[72] *Ibid.*

[73] *Ibid.*, 229.

[74] Shiner, *Follow Me!* 227.

[75] *Ibid.*, 232.

[76] *Ibid.*, 264.

[77] Craig A. Evans, "*Mark 8:1-16:20*", in ed. Bruce M. Metzger, WBC, vol. 34B (Dallas, Texas: Word Publishing, 1989), 264.

[78] Craig, *Mark 8:1-16:20*, 264.

[79] Behm, "καρδια," in *TDNT*, ed. Gerhard Kittel, vol. III (Grand Rapids, Michigan: Eerdmans, 1965), 607.

[80] *Ibid.*, 608.

[81] *Ibid.*

[82] νους was naively used in the synoptic tradition (only once in Lk. 24:45). This as Behm rightly suggested could only be possible under the assumption that primitive Christianity stood quite apart from the philosophical reflection and religious mysticism of the surrounding world. (Behm, "νοεω," in *TDNT*, ed. Gerhard Kittel, vol. IV (Grand Rapids, Michigan: Eerdmans, 1965), 960.

[83] *Ibid.*, 963.

[84] *Ibid.*

[85] *Ibid.*, 965.

[86] Evans, *Mark 8:1-16:20*, 264.

[87] B. Bandstra and S. S Stuart, "Mind," in *The International Standard Bible Encyclopedia*, ed. Geoffrey W. Bromiley, vol. III (Grand Rapids, Michigan: Eerdmans, 1986), 362.

[88] Ezra P. Gould. *Mark,* The International Critical Commentary (Edinburgh: T&T Clark, 1982), 232.

[89] This is clear as Witherington has highlighted that Mark goes to explain certain Aramaic terms and Jewish customs. (Witherington, *Rhetoric,* 26.)

[90] Marcus, "Mark 4:10-12," 573.

CHAPTER 2

The Role of the Mind in Matthean Discipleship

In their uncompromising determination to proclaim truth, Christians must avoid the intellectual flabbiness of the larger society. They must rally against the prevailing distrust of reason and the exaltation of the irrational. Emotional self-indulgence and irrationalities have always been the enemies of the Gospel, and the apostles warned their followers against them.

                                                    –Herbert Schlossberg[1]

Introduction

This chapter explores the role of understanding in discipleship as Matthew portrays it. Interestingly, Matthew paints a much more positive picture of the disciples than Mark.[2] So, instead of being those who fail to comprehend, in Matthew, Jesus' disciples are presented as those who comprehended. However, it does not mean that the two Gospel accounts are contradictory. This is because the evangelists write in different environments.[3] It is precisely for this reason that studying the nature of Matthew's immediate audience becomes significant for our present research. It will also be discovered that in contrast to Mark, in Matthew, the disciples have gained understanding about Jesus' true identity and their focus is centred on his instructions[4] As the wisdom motif is developed in this Gospel,[5] which is relevant to our present study, we shall also discuss "wisdom" in this Gospel. This leads to our discussion on the theme of comprehension in Matthew as portrayed by Matthew. Unlike the previous chapter, this chapter attempts to trace the epistemological understanding of Matthew's Gospel subsequent to the discussion on the theme of comprehension.

Nature of the Matthean Community

The Matthean community was a segregated Jewish community with   few Gentile converts.[6] This community lived in the post-Temple period probably in 80-90 CE. However, just like the issue of authorship,[7] any clear-cut decision about the date of writing[8] of the Gospel cannot be made. Carter observes evidence[9] within the text that points to Syrian Antioch as the place of writing. Keener[10] and Sim[11] also hold a similar view.

Regarding the nature of the community, Stanton perceives it as an institution closely related to and in opposition to the Jewish synagogue from which it had recently parted.[12] The fact of ongoing persecution is evident as Sim shows how the mission of the Matthean community entailed an inevitable contact[13] with the leadership of formative Judaism, which, in turn, involved persecution (Mt. 10:22) and the risk of death (10:28, 31, 39).[14] In one of the redacted passages, Matthew extends the list of crimes committed by the Jewish religious leaders: They killed and crucified some, while others they scourged in the synagogue and persecuted from town to town (23:29-36).[15]

According to Carter, the cause of persecution was the community's claim that Jesus truly interprets the Old Testament tradition, that he truly manifests God's saving presence and empire[16] and that Jesus is the supreme eschatological agent of God's revelation.[17] Chapter 10 gives indication of the persecution of the community by the Gentiles, where Matthew shares about their mistreatment by the Gentiles (10:18).[18]

Another interesting issue is the possible effect of the Temple destruction on the community. Carter shows that within the post-destruction debate about God's ensuing presence, the Matthean community made distinctive claims[19] about Jesus, whom they had experienced.[20] In this light, it is reasonable to think that during the time of the composition of this Gospel, the community was disillusioned and was struggling to make sense of life in the light of their pain and hostility.[21]

Portrait of Matthean Discipleship

Matthew points to three groups, which are present everywhere in the Gospel: (1) the disciples, (2) the crowds and (3) the teachers of the law and the Pharisees.[22] Kingsbury says that Matthew differentiates between them by showing whether, or to what extent, different characters understand Jesus' teachings and rightly respond by obeying them (i.e., doing God's will, 12:49-50).[23] Matthew paints a picture of true disciples–through depicting the right responses (of his characters) in contrast to the wrong ones. In other words, Matthew contrasts the true disciples with the false ones based on their obedient responses to Jesus and his teachings. Even when the disciples faltered and failed at times, Matthew shows that in the end they do understand and obey Jesus' instructions (16:12; 17:13, 23; 28:17a).[24] In contrast to the disciples, the crowds (13:10-17, 34-36) and the Jewish leaders ultimately reject Jesus, the Son of God (9:34; 12:14; 21:18-19, 41-43; 22:7; 23:37-39; 24:15; 27:25).

Based on Mt. 11:29, Luz believes that Matthew conveys that people attain God's grace through obedience—a human activity.[25] In line with this view, Riches says that Matthew lays a greater emphasis on human responsibility in God's overall plan of salvation.[26] Thus, Kingsbury rightly defines discipleship as the life of a person who in "seeing" and "hearing" Jesus amid the events of the story, "understands" him aright thereby making an adequate response by "receiving him" and "doing" God's will as he teaches it.[27]

Thus, in Matthew, the mark of a true disciple is a correct understanding[28] about Jesus and his instructions, which leads to an obedient response. Likewise, the community is exhorted to continue to apply their minds to understand Jesus' instructions in order to bear fruit for the kingdom of God (13:19a).

Nature of Matthew's Gospel

Based upon 1:23 and 28:20, Kingsbury sees Jesus as being the focus of the entire story of Matthew's Gospel. He views Matthew's central thesis as follows: "In the person of Jesus Christ, the Son of God, God has drawn near to abide with his people, the church, thus inaugurating the eschatological age of salvation."[29] The viewpoints of Matthew that shed light on the obvious theme of comprehension in this Gospel are:

* Apocalyptic
* Deterministic view of history
* Epistemological

Apocalyptic

Sim says that in agreement with the Qumran Scroll and the book of Revelation, Matthew writes with an apocalyptic view and presents the supernatural world as a realm of cosmic struggle between God and his agents, on one hand, and Satan and his agents, on the other.[30] In Matthew 11:27b, Matthew presents Jesus as God's revelation, and knowledge of him can only be received as God's gift from above. Luz rightly says that Matthew is aware of a Christology "from above."[31]

Regarding human existence, Sim asserts that it represents the cosmic struggle, which is clearly evident in the parable of the tares in 13:36-43.[32] Through their faith and obedient response to Jesus, Matthew depicts the disciples to be on the side of God, while the Jewish leaders[33] and Rome (4:8) belong to the side of Satan. Thus, as Sim suggests, for Matthew the human world is fundamentally divided into good and evil, and each group is aligned with its cosmic counterpart.[34]

Deterministic view of History

Matthew also says that God has determined in advance the course of history up to and beyond the turn of eras.[35] This is clearly evident in 22:14, where Matthew presents the notion of pre-selection.[36] This deterministic view of history is also evident in the fulfillment motif, in which none of the New Testament authors were as interested as Matthew is.[37] The "fulfillment motif" would have helped Matthew in asserting that just as Jesus' prophecies concerning the present are fulfilled, those predictions of Jesus concerning the "eschaton" will surely meet with fulfillment.[38]

Thus, Matthew presents world history as in God's total control. In line with this, Carter says that Matthew urges the audience to live an alternative, subversive and patient existence shaped by God's empire and in anticipation of its full establishment in God's final salvation.[39]

Epistemological
In his apocalyptic tone, Matthew aims to provide an understanding to the readers about the ongoing earthly events. He shows that the visible events are not the ultimate reality. Rather, they are an outcome of hidden activities of the unseen world–the ongoing cosmic struggle. In a context of rejection and persecution, the Gospel story provides a symbolic universe, a context for making sense of its past, a direction to shape its present and future.[40] In this way, Matthew's Gospel acts as an epistemic window that helped the disciples to make sense of the present difficulties and exhorted them to make an appropriate response of believing and obeying Jesus. This appropriate response, as Matthew's Gospel implies, is possible for those who apply their minds to understand Jesus' teachings to follow him.[41]

Wisdom in Matthew
Matthew personifies Jesus as wisdom incarnate.[42] Based on 11:25-30, France argues for Matthew's awareness of wisdom ideas that he deliberately uses in order to draw out the significance of Jesus as one through whom God speaks.[43] Moreover, Matthew says that the wisdom that Jesus brings is not based on human intellect but on God's act of grace.[44] However, Jesus' wisdom has a paradox. Rather than it being the wise people of the world making an

appropriate response to Jesus, it is the children and insignificant people who make an obedient response, thus making them wiser than the wise of the world. There is an element of reversal in Matthew's portrayal of the truly wise.

Barton says that wisdom is a way of seeing, which attends to what lies hidden, as well as to what lies on the surface.[45] Since the Gospels present Jesus as Wisdom incarnate and as one who provides the measure of what constitutes wisdom[46] Barton rightly says that "true wisdom is one that is understood in relation to Christ and the cross."[47] He also says that Jesus gives access to this wisdom both by his invitation (11:27-28) and by exemplifying it in his life (12:15-21).[48]

Commenting on the "rest" mentioned in Jesus' call to follow him in 11:28, Barton says that it points to an eschatological rest.[49] Moreover, 11:28-30 also asserts that the promise of rest for the "simple ones" is because unlike the Pharisees, they learn from Jesus. Thus, Matthew implies that the truly wise are only those who accept Jesus and his teachings made evident by an obedient response.

Matthean Theme of Comprehension

As noted before, Matthew writes with the conviction that Jesus is the "Son of God" (1:23; 2:11; 3:14,17; 8:6, 29; 14:33; 28:17), who truly interprets and fulfills the Torah (5:17). In a similar vein, Wilkins says that through his Gospel, Matthew aims to present the fulfillment of God's redeeming motive and activity in the person of Christ.[50] Unlike Mark, for Matthew, the disciples have gained an understanding of Jesus (14:33[51]) and the focus of their understanding is shifted to his parables and instructions,[52] which they finally understand (16:12; 17:13, 23; 28:17a).

Based on the parable of the soil, it is clear that a proper understanding of Jesus' instruction is inevitable for and proven through fruit bearing (13:23). Thus, Luz rightly says that in Matthew, "understanding" is more than an act of intellectual grasp of Jesus' teachings. It means realising what a word signifies to oneself, holding on to that realisation and putting it into practice.[53]

Purpose of the Theme of Comprehension

The theme of the disciples' incomprehension is less obvious in Matthew than in Mark. Overman shows how Matthew omits Mark 9:6,10 and 32, all of which speak of the Markan motif of the failure to perceive, and in contrast Matthew makes explicit claims that the disciples do indeed understand or come close to understanding (13:51; 15:16ff; 16:9-12; 17: 13).[54] This is because Matthew shows the disciples as comprehending ones and as instructors of the Word of God (in contrast to the Jewish religious authorities).[55] Kingsbury sees that the disciples' story serves the larger purpose of enabling Jesus to instruct the disciples or to mediate new insight to them.[56] This corroborates with the fact that Jesus is portrayed as an authoritative and effective teacher.[57] Matthew shows the disciples as models for the Matthean community.[58] In this way, Matthew utilises the disciples' comprehension to encourage his community to fully understand the teachings of Jesus and to apply them.[59] In this way, the disciples' incomprehension acts as a foil for the presentation of Jesus' teachings so that his community could understand them.

Thematic Study of Comprehension

Based on the phrase "from that time on" found in 4:17 and 16:21, Kingsbury[60] and France[61] present the story of Matthew in three major sections.[62] Regarding these divisions, France also adds that each of the two pointers serve not so much to mark out end of a theme as to move the story onto the next phase of its development.[63] As noted before, Matthew differentiates between true and false disciples by showing whether, or to what extent, different characters understand Jesus' teachings and accordingly respond by obeying them. Since human responses are dependent on the underlying understanding, in portraying the various responses to Jesus, Matthew is emphasising the critical need of understanding Jesus and his instructions aright in order to make an obedient response. The motif of comprehension is thus discernible through the various human responses to Jesus in Matthew's Gospel.

The human responses to Jesus are evident right from the early part of the Matthean plot. In the first section (1:1-4:16), Matthew portrays the responses of Joseph and the Magi with approval (1:24; 2:21 and 2:11), in contrast to that of Herod (2:16), who sought to kill baby Jesus. In the second and largest section (4:17-16:20), Jewish religious leaders take Herod's place as tensions between Jesus and Jewish religious leaders increase and ultimately lead them to crucify Jesus.[64] The crowds follow Jesus only in a literal sense.[65] This is clear in that, after having received Jesus' instructions and having become excited (4:25; 5:1; 7:28-29; 9:23-25; 11: 20-24; 15:30-31), in the end they reject Jesus (cf. 27:22-23).

The disciples, however, are shown in a positive light (Mt.5:1b; 10:1; 11:1; 12:7; 12:49-50; 16:12; 16:16).[66] In the Matthean plot, Luz shows that chapter 11 intrudes abruptly into the thread of Matthew's story.[67] He suggests that chapter 11, represents a backward glance and summing up of the ensuing rejection of Jesus by the Jews.[68] This is clear because at this point the crowds are still friendly and receptive toward Jesus. The community of those to whom the secret of the Son and the Father is to be revealed has not yet come into existence.[69]

In the third section (16:21-28:20), when he predicts his death on a cross, the disciples appear to be in conflict with Jesus as Peter refuses to believe Jesus (16:22; see also 19:13; 20:28). This resistance to accept that Jesus must suffer and his suffering constitute a summons to suffering discipleship. It led them to the point of betraying Jesus (26:47-50, 56, 69-75). In spite of this, Jesus continues to instruct them privately.[70] In the end, the disciples come to accept Jesus' evaluative point of view, concerning both Jesus himself (26:32 cf. 28:5-10) and concerning themselves (28:18-20).

In a series of three parables (21:28-22:10), Matthew characterises the religious leaders in a programmatic fashion as having not received but "repudiated" the eschatological agents that God had sent: John the Baptist, Jesus himself and the disciples, (who act as missionaries). Regarding this, Kingsbury rightly says that through these parables, Jesus summons the readers to adopt his theological point of view and his understanding.[71]

Chapters 26-28 show how the Jewish leaders apparently asserted themselves against Jesus. Luz shows how the Gospel ends with two antithetic pericopae. On one side are the "Jews" (28:15), who to this day cannot comprehend the truth about Jesus. On the other side, is the resurrected Lord, who, from the mountaintop in Galilee, sends forth his disciples to the Gentiles (28:19-20).[72]

In this way, Matthew depicts a historical progression of a dual response of the disciples and the Jewish leaders to Jesus and his teachings, where the disciples' responses are depicted with approval while that of other Jews with disapproval. Thus, Matthew exhorts the readers to "hear" and to "understand" in order to follow Jesus as the disciples did.

Matthean Epistemology and Matthean Community

In 11:25-26 and 13:11-12, Jesus sees revelation to a few as a result of God's will to conceal his revelation from Israel and reveal it to the disciples' "infants." This raises a question about God's justice. Commenting upon the repudiation of Israel in chapter 11, Luz says that it bears witness to Israel's incomprehensible obstinacy: its lack of understanding, the grossness of heart, its inability to hear, its eyes shut tight to keep from seeing.[73] Luz asserts this by pointing at Israel's guilt: they closed their eyes so as not to hear or see, otherwise God would truly heal them.[74] This is plausible as Luz rightly argues that Matthew writes for a post-Easter persecuted community, having the conviction about God's absolute control over the human race.

Matthew reconciles Jesus' rejection by the Jews and God's absolute sovereignty by encouraging the community to interpret their present ongoing persecution in the light of Isaiah 6:9-10.[75] Thus, Matthew points to human hard-heartedness, unwillingness and inaptitude as factors that keep some out of God's revelation.

The above discussion implies that God does not actively hide his mysteries from some. On the contrary, the mysteries of God have been given to those who have a receptive and perceptive disposition. Luz points to the inevitable need for God's action in the disciples' understanding and says that mysteries are comprehensible only by the Father alone (16:17).[76] Based on this, Luz rightly argues that the "simple ones" mentioned in 11:28, do not participate like disembodied spirits in the extraordinary, mystical reciprocal awareness between Father and Son, but rather they "learn" from Jesus to travel a very specific path.[77]

Thus, the special quality of the disciples (and the community) lies merely in the fact that they hear and understand the words of Jesus (13:51; 16:12; 17:23), i.e., they have Jesus as their teacher, and He instructs them until they have comprehended the mysteries of the Kingdom of God. Like Mark, Matthew presents the mysteries of the Kingdom in the form of parables (chapter 13). Parables reveal basic reality to the disciples (though hidden from Israel) that the end time Kingdom of God confronts people in the person of Jesus and will culminate in Jesus' final judgment at the end of the age (13:31-32).

While Matthew presents the disciples as those who understand, he remains sensitive to their historical value. Thus, Matthew shows the weaknesses of the disciples as they follow Jesus and which lead them into conflict with Jesus.[78] The reason for this conflict could be explained in terms of Matthew's parable of the Sower. In this parable, the influences acting on the first three kinds of soils (13:19-22) inhibited the growth of those who ventured on the path of discipleship.

The above point is further clarified as Matthew picks up on the theme of blindness again and again (Mt. 9:27-31; 12:22-24; 20:29-34; 21:14), which represents the community's experience of being led by Jesus from blindness to knowledge (about his identity and true meaning of the day-to-day events).[79] Luz argues that in Matthew, "blindness" had a literal nuance and was meant to be unenlightened or to live under the darkness of the old aeon.[80] Thus,

Matthew emphasises that it is Jesus who brings complete enlightenment and, therefore, all are called to accept him and follow his teachings. It is only then that the community as well as humanity at large will be able to understand the real nature and significance of everyday events.

Conclusion

Matthew's Gospel is the story of Jesus, whom he presents as God's promised Son. This is evident in the "fulfillment" motif. Regarding "understanding", Matthew shows that while knowing Jesus is a gift from above, it takes human initiative to understand Jesus' instruction. This is clear from the parable of the sower as well as Jesus' call to learn from him in chapter 11. Further, Matthew exhorts his hearers to understand Jesus' instructions aright by depicting authentic and inauthentic ways of responding to Jesus. From his apocalyptic position, Matthew presents how earthly events are an outcome of a cosmic struggle, which will come to an end in the decisive defeat of Satan and his allies during the eschatological judgment. This would help the community to understand the ongoing persecution and ill treatment by fellow Jews.

Matthew also develops the wisdom motif and presents Jesus as "wisdom incarnate." Through this, Matthew shows that those who follow Jesus are the truly wise, and thereby he exhorts his community of disciples to make an appropriate response by applying their minds to understand and follow Jesus.

End Notes

[1] Quoted in J. P. Moreland, *Love Your God with All Your Mind: The Role of Reason in the Life of the Soul* (Colorado, Colorado Springs: Navpress, 1997), 85.

[2] While in Mark the disciples frequently failed to comprehend Jesus and his teachings, in Matthew the disciples are portrayed as well taught learners in the way of wisdom. (Wilkins, *Following*, 180; Andrew J. Overman, *Matthew's Gospel and Formative Judaism: The Social World of Matthean Community* (Minneapolis: Fortress, 1990),128; Stephen C. Barton, "Gospel Wisdom," in *Where Shall Wisdom be Found*, ed. Stephen C. Barton (Edinburgh: T&T Clark, 1999), 95; and   Ulrich Luz, *The*

Theology of the Gospel of Matthew, NTT (Cambridge: Cambridge University Press, 1993), 92.

[3] Overman shows how Matthew's portrayal of the disciples is one crucial place where the setting and situation of the Matthean community has dramatically influenced the shape and the content of the Gospel. Overman, *Matthew's Gospel,* 125.

[4] Ulrich Luz, "The Disciples in the Gospel according to Matthew," in *The Interpretation of Matthew,* ed. Graham Stanton (Edinburgh: T&T Clark, 1995), 121.

[5] Barton, "Gospel Wisdom," 94.

[6] The Gentile presence within the community is plausible in light of the fact that Matthew is not against all people of non-Jewish background. Thus, Matthew aimed to emphasize that it is commitment to Jesus and not ethnic descent from Abraham that provides basis for God's people (12:50; 21:43; 22:7). Sim makes a similar point through the final command of Jesus in 28:19, which acknowledges that certain Gentiles can be viewed with approval. David C. Sim, *Apocalyptic Eschatology in the Gospel of Matthew,* SNTS Mon. Ser., 88 (Cambridge: Cambridge University Press, 1996), 208.

[7] Regarding Authorship, Carter says that in all likelihood, it was not the disciple Matthew named in 9:9. Warren Carter, *Matthew and the Margins: A Socio-Political and Religious Reading,* JSNT Suppl. Ser., 204 (Sheffield: Sheffield Academic Press, 2000), 14. This is because Carter in line with Keener sees that the gospel was written a decade or two after the destruction of the temple. Craig S. Keener, *Matthew,* The IVP New Testament Commentary Series (Leicester: IVP, 1997), 33. Carter says that it is unlikely that the original disciple Matthew would have lived by then (an era in which age forty was considered old). Carter, *Matthew,* 14. However, for the sake of convenience, I shall be using the conventional name of 'Matthew' for our study.

[8] Regarding the date of writing, Carter presents a very realistic equation that favors a date in the eighties or nineties. He does so by relating Matthew's gospel to chronological events in the last quarter of first century and the first quarter of the second century. *Ibid.*

[9] Carter says that reference to Syria in 4:24 is Matthean redaction as it is absent in its parallel in Mk. 1:28, 39 and also as Galilee is the point of emphasis in the context of chapter four (4:12-15, 23, 25). Carter sees it an act of giving local color to the story of Jesus, *Ibid.,* 15. There is a greater emphasis on Peter in Matthew than in Mark. Carter sees this as a pointer to Syrian origin of Matthew's gospel. This is so in the light of the significant role that Peter played in the Antiochian church (Gal. 2:11-14). *Ibid.,* 16.

[10] Keener, *Matthew*, 33.

[11] Sim, *Gospel*, 10.

[12] Sim also quotes Stanton who argues against the view that Matthean community still considered itself proponents of Judaism (21:43 and 28:15). Sim, *Gospel*, 2.

[13] On why would the community have gone to a resistant Jews, Sim explains that anything less would have been a betrayal of the Petrine mission, which the community inherited. (Sim, *Matthew*, 162.)

[14] Sim, *Gospel*, 58.

[15] *Ibid.*

[16] This corresponded to numerous documents of the post 70 CE era (viz. in the name of figures like Abraham, Enoch, Mosses, Baruch, Ezra and Solomon) that claimed definitive revelations and teachings. (Carter, *Matthew*, 36.)

[17] Jack Dean Kingsbury, "The Rhetoric of Comprehension in the Gospel of Matthew," *NTS* 41 (1995): 359.

[18] Matthew 10:18- "On my account you will be brought before governors and kings as witnesses to them and to the Gentiles".

[19] These claims are: (a) Jesus forgives sin (establishing it even before his birth, Mt. 1:21); (b) Jesus manifests God's presence (Mt. 1:23; 25: 31-46; 28:18-20); (c)Jesus interprets God's will (Mt. 9:11-13; 11:10; 12:1-8, 9-14; 13:14-17; 15:1-20; 19:3-12; 22:34-40; 22:41-46). Carter, *Matthew*, 34-36.

[20] *Ibid.*, 33.

[21] *Ibid.*

[22] Michael Green, *The Message of Matthew*. BST (Leicester, England: IVP, 2000), 29.

[23] Kingsbury, "Rhetoric of Comprehension," 359.

[24] Michael J. Wilkins, *Following the Master: Discipleship in the Steps of Jesus* (Grand Rapids, Michigan: Zondervan, 1992), 180.

[25] Luz, *Theology*, 96.

[26] John K. Riches, *Conflicting Mythologies: Identity Formation in the Gospel of Mark and Matthew*. Studies of the New Testament and Its World (Edinburgh: T&T Clark, 2000), 315.

[27] Kingsbury, "Rhetoric of Comprehension," 359.

[28] Wilkins says that Matthew more than any other evangelist emphasizes that the essence of true discipleship lies in understanding and obeying Jesus' teaching. Wilkins, *Following the Master*, 181.

[29] Jack Dean Kingsbury, *Matthew as a Story*, 2d. ed. (Philadelphia: Fortress, 1988), 42.

[30] Sim, *Apocalyptic*, 75.

[31] Luz, *Theology*, 99.

[32] Sim, *Apocalyptic*, 78. In this parable, Son of Man sows the good seed, which represent the sons of the kingdom, while the weeds which arise amidst the seed are the sons of the evil one and are sown by none other than Satan, who is the chief enemy (v. 37-39a). (Sim, *Apocalyptic*, 79.)

[33] Though the gospel of Matthew has a conservative Jewish tone, Matthew treats the Jewish religious leaders as one homogenous force that is totally united in opposition to Jesus, thereby depicting them as the real villains, whom Matthew singles out as being evil (9:4; 12:34; 22:18). Sim, *Apocalyptic*, 184.

[34] This is further clear when unlike Luke (who talks about entering by a narrow door), Matthew talks about not one point of entry, but two doors that lead to two different destinations (see also 112:36-37; 13:47-50). *Ibid.*, 83.

[35] France shows several views regarding the eras in salvation history (e.g. G. Strecker, who views three stages in history of salvation; Kingsbury and Donaldson and Luz, who views two stages). I agree with France who says that speaking in terms of definable stages of *Heilsgeshichte* reflects a modern desire to systematize Matthew's thought, which seems more akin to the atmosphere of Dispensationalism than to any obvious concern of the evangelist himself. France, *Matthew*, 199.

Contra Strecker, France takes his stand with Luz's transparency principle, and stands close to the two-stage view of salvation history. The first stage is the age of prophecy. The second is the age of fulfillment or better known as the eschatological age inaugurated in the coming of Jesus Christ. He goes on to point that for Matthew, though the past remains past, it was in the real events and teaching of pre-Easter Jesus that Matthew saw fulfillment taking place. And it is to those same real events and teaching of the past that the post Easter church must continue to look for. *Ibid.*, 201.

[36] The pericope concludes with the words, "for many are called but only few are chosen", Mt. 22: 14. Sim, *Apocalyptic*, 87.

[37] The fulfillment motif is spread throughout the Gospel: Mt. 3:3; 11:19; 15:7-9; 21:42; 26:56 and unique to Matthew, Mt. 26: 54. *Ibid.*, 88.

[38] *Ibid.*, 90.

[39] Carter, *Matthew and the Margins*, 37.

[40] Carter, *Matthew and the Margins*, 33.

[41] Overman asserts a similar point when he says that the disciples in Matthew are called to understand and instruct. Overman, *Matthew's Gospel*, 133.

[42] James D. G. Dunn, "Where Shall Wisdom Be Found," in *Where Shall Wisdom Be Found*, ed. Stephen C. Barton (Edinburgh: T&T Clark, 1999), 92. See also Sugg's view in France, *Matthew*, 304-05.

[43] *Ibid.*, 305.

[44] Based on Mt. 11:25-30, Barton suggests that divine wisdom is the fruit of being in filial relationship with God and is not an outcome of solitary intellection [sic]. Barton, *Gospel Wisdom*, 96.

[45] *Ibid.*, 94.

[46] *Ibid.*

[47] Barton sees that Matthew presents this theme right in the beginning by depicting wise men from the East (2:1-18), which is paradigmatic of the fact that the ancient quest of the nations for wisdom and of the revelation of wisdom finds its fulfillment in baby Jesus. *Ibid.*, 94-95.

[48] *Ibid.*, 98.

[49] Barton argues this based on the fact that Jesus' invitation to 'rest' in 11:28 in immediately followed by two controversy stories about the Sabbath (12:1-8, 9-14). *Ibid.*

[50] Wilkins, *Following the Master*, 181.

[51] See the parallel account in Mk. 6:45-52, where the disciples do not understand Jesus' identity as their hearts were hardened.

[52] Ulrich Luz, "The Disciples in the Gospel according to Matthew" in *The Interpretation of Matthew*, ed. Graham N. Stanton, Studies in the New Testament Interpretation (Edinburg: T&T Clark, 1983), 121. Kingsbury also says that the disciples come into conflict with Jesus not primarily in regard to Jesus' identity, but in adopting his evaluative point of view as servanthood. (Kingsbury, *Matthew as a Story*, 104)

[53] Luz, *Theology*, 93.

[54] Overman, *Matthew's*, 128.

[55] This portrayal of the disciples would thus defend the community's life and order from attacks from the authorities outside the community who challenge their beliefs. *Ibid.*, 134.

[56] Kingsbury, *Matthew as a Story*, 139.

[57] Overman, *Matthew's*, 127.

[58] *Ibid.*, 135.

[59] *Ibid.*

[60] Kingsbury, *Matthew as a Story*, 43. He presents this outline based upon Matthew's usage of the stereotyped phrase, "from that time on" at 4:16 and 16:21 (that mark two important turns in Matthew's story about Jesus). *Ibid.*, 40.

[61] Regarding the structure France says that both the geographical location

and the style of Jesus' ministry changes radically at 4:16 and 16:20 and therefore, there is no reason to doubt that Matthew intended the use of phrase 'from that time on' to mark the fact. France, *Matthew*, 152.

[62] Section one (1:1- 4:16), divinely attests the 'identity of Jesus' (Mt. 3:17), a motif that dominates in the early part of Matthew's story. Second section (4:17-16:20), deals with two main themes. In the first part 4:17-11:1, Matthew tells of the ministry of Jesus to Israel (4:23-27 cf. 9:35-38 summary statements; chapter 5-7; 11:1 – teaching ministry; 8-9 – healing ministry) and in conjunction with this, of the call of the disciples (4:18-22) and of their mission (chapter 10). The second part 11:2-16:20 tells about Israel's repudiation of Jesus (11:20-24) and how the disciples in contrast stand out as recipients of divine revelation (11:25-30). The third section, 16:21-28:20 tells about Jesus' journey to Jerusalem, his passion and resurrection.

[63] *Ibid.*, 153.

[64] Mt. 9: 33b-34; 12:14; 24; 12:38; 15:1; 16:1. See also 19:3; 21:13, 23f; 22:5, 15, chapter 23; 26:3, 65-66; 27:20, 41.

[65] Wilkins, Follow Me, 179.

[66] Except in 8:26-27, where they fail to exercise their faith in Jesus. However, Matthew improves upon this by differing from Mark in the second boat scene, where the disciples understand Jesus' true being and bow down to worship him (Mt. 14:32-33 cf. Mk. 6:51-52).

[67] Luz, *Theology*, 63.

[68] *Ibid.*, 65.

[69] *Ibid.*, 81.

[70] 16:21-20:34 records the life of the new community formed as a result of withdrawals – the church. See also 18:1; 23:1; 24:1-3, where Jesus addresses the disciples primarily to prevent their lives from becoming like those of 'religious authorities' that were characterised by hypocrisy and hunger for honour.

[71] Kingsbury, "Rhetoric of Comprehension," 370.

[72] Luz, *Theology*, 65.

[73] *Ibid.*, 98.

[74] *Ibid.*, 98.

[75] *Ibid.*, 99.

[76] *Ibid.*, 99

[77] *Ibid.*, 99.

[78] *Ibid.*, 138.

[79] *Ibid.*

[80] Luz, *Theology*, 68.

CHAPTER 3

The Role of the Mind in Lukan Discipleship

We are having a revival of feelings but not of the knowledge of God. The church today is guided more by feelings rather than by conviction. We value enthusiasm more than informed commitment.

—1980 Gallup Poll on Religion[1]

Introduction

Like Matthew, Luke also presents us with a fairly positive picture of the disciples. This is evident as Luke does not have the passages like Mark 4:13; 6:50-52 and 8:17-21 (regarding the disciples' inaptitude and hard-heartedness). The disciples are also distinct from all others in that they leave everything else to follow Jesus (14:26-27, 33) and to hear and obey his words (6:47-48 cf. v.20). However, there are occasions when the disciples failed to understand or thus misunderstood the identity and purpose of Jesus (8:25; 9:44-45; 18:31-34). This chapter aims to explore the role of understanding in discipleship as Luke portrays it. To this end, we will take a look at the context of Luke's writing and his audience. Then, we will explore Luke's portrait of discipleship. This will be followed by looking at the nature of Luke's Gospel. This follows the study of disciples' incomprehension. The chapter concludes with a study of the Lukan epistemological framework and its bearing on his community (readers).

Nature of Lukan Community

In this chapter, we have attempted to trace a picture of the Lukan community. Through this, we believe, we can better understand the original context of the writing of Luke's Gospel and, in turn, his distinctive view on discipleship. Based on the amount of detail that Luke-Acts[2] has devoted to faithfulness, Jewish-Gentile relations and clinging to the hope of Jesus' return, Bock sees Theophilus as a Gentile who was experiencing doubt about his association with the new community;[3] a community that was originally a Jewish movement, but was also under intense pressure from the Jews.[4] Doohan sees this community in a similar way: it was continuously under criticism that was undermining the confidence in the future of the "Way" and had cast doubt on the truth concerning "the things of which they were instructed."[5]

Based on the great Lukan effort in writing the Gospel (and Acts), Bock suggests that he did not write for Theophilus alone but for many who shared his doubts about being part of the new community of believers.[6]

Commenting upon Luke's audience, Forbes sees them as a group of God fearers. He also sees Luke's purpose was evangelistic proclamation apart from discipleship instruction.[7] The above evidence suggests that Luke's audience was a mixed community that probably lived in a Jewish context and was undergoing persecution.[8] Bock sees that for a Gentile, Luke's Gospel would have provided reassurance in an originally Jewish movement. While on the other hand, for a Jew it would have explained the Jewish rejection of the Gospel in the light of God's multiple invitations in his renewed work.[9]

Nolland points to the Temple loyalty in Luke, which is clear as Luke restates the anticipation of judgment with a focus on Jerusalem and not so much on the temple (19:41-44; 21:20-24).[10] While Nolland uses this data to argue for a pre-70 CE date for Luke's composition, the same could be used to argue for a post-70 CE date of composition.[11] Thus, based on Lukan redaction of the phrase "the desolating sacrilege", in Mark 13:14 to "when you see Jerusalem surrounded by armies.... " in Lk. 21:20, Tuckett argues for a late 70s CE as the date of composition of Luke's Gospel.[12] Moreover, since Luke used Mark as one of his sources,13 it is reasonable to conclude that Luke wrote in the post-Temple era.

Lukan Portrait of Discipleship

Luke presents us with various groups of the disciples, depending on their intimacy with Jesus. At the innermost circle are the two sets of brothers (Peter and Andrew and James and John). Then come the twelve, who are followed by the seventy, and then the women who ministered to Jesus. In the last circle of the disciples, came the crowd, who were very curious about Jesus and his ministry but who had not yet believed.[14] This description is significant to understand the Lukan view of discipleship.[15] Based on this, Luke shows that not everyone who follows or confesses Jesus has made a decision.[16] This explains Jesus' exhortation to make every effort to enter through the narrow gate[17] (13:23-24). Based on 22:67, Beck observes that the basic disposition of faith (that results in salvation) involves the assent of the will (cf. 20:5; Acts 5:32).[18]

Luke presents discipleship through the "journey motif"[19] as following "the Way" (Acts 18:24-25; cf. e.g., Luke 1:6; 20:21).[20] This is evident as Luke develops his geographical perspective, with Jerusalem at the centre, towards which Jesus journeys for the Passion (9:51), and the disciples traveling with him along the road (v. 57). Based on the journey motif, Doohan, in agreement with Green,[21] sees that since following Jesus is a continuous commitment of the disciples, faith (conversion) is an ongoing reality, which is indistinguishable from discipleship.[22] Marshall makes a similar point while commenting on 8:12-13.[23] Nolland says that the disciples are those who have left everything (5:11, 28; 14:26-27, 33) and those who not only hear, but also do all that Jesus says (Lk. 6:47 cf. v.20).[24]

While Jesus extends an open invitation to all, he also points to the need of making an assessment before venturing into discipleship. This is because genuine discipleship is costly. Wilkins sees that the theme of "counting the cost" provides a summary for Luke's overall portrait of discipleship (e.g. 9:57-62; 18:24-30).[25] He sees two nuances to it. Positively, it meant that one's heart, soul, mind and strength must be focused on loving God and one's neighbor as oneself (10:27-28). Negatively, it meant that one entered into the life of discipleship through detaching oneself from competing allegiances and giving personal allegiance to Jesus as Master.[26] This is clear as Pilgrim says how the disciples had adopted a life of poverty by deliberate choice and by virtue of their call of the Kingdom.[27] Through a well-known example like Peter, Luke shows that promises are easy to make but the cost must be counted in advance (cf. 14:28f).[28]

Thus, in the context of following Jesus on his way to Jerusalem, Luke shows how counting the cost not only meant the cost of what discipleship meant, but also the cost of what completing the process of discipleship would mean (14:28-33) in everyday living.[29] Commenting on Luke 9:23f, Nolland says that radical commitment is not something that is called for only in crisis situations; but it is a commitment that needs to be renewed daily, one that needs to undergird all that happens in our daily lives.[30]

The commitment of each disciple must not only be to understanding Jesus' words, but also to obeying Jesus' teachings.[31] Thus, Lukan discipleship is built on the foundation of obedience (e.g. the wise and foolish builders in 6:47).

Nature of Luke's Gospel

Bock convincingly presents three main issues that place this Gospel in the post-Temple destruction era.[32] While various aims of Luke have been suggested, Bock sees three ideas as most likely to reflect Luke's most comprehensive agenda: Firstly, to confirm the Word and the message of salvation (van Unnik, Marshall, O'Toole); secondly, to present a theodicy of God's faithfulness (Tiede); and thirdly, to provide a sociological legitimation of full fellowship for Gentiles and a defense of the new community (Esler).[33] In certain places, Luke sets out the same facts as Mark, but the difference is in the manner, depending on the audience (e.g. Lk. 9:18 cf. Mk. 8:27). While each of the above views have their own arguments, we go along with the first view as we believe that Luke's primary concern was to present a systematic account of the soteriological significance of the life and ministry of Jesus.

Theme of Incomprehension

Conzelmann rightly sees that Luke turns the Jesus enigma into incomprehension and misunderstanding of his passion.[34] Similarly, Kingsbury sees that their failure to understand is principally in regards to Jesus' passion.[35] In line with Conzelmann and Kingsbury, Green sees that Luke primarily relates all these failures to the disciples' inability to fully understand Jesus' impending suffering and death (9:21-27. 44-45).[36] Thus, in Luke, the theme of incomprehension is underlined as the disciples do not even understand the upcoming passion of Jesus (9:45). This is clear, as the disciples do not protest about the way that lies ahead of Jesus[37] and as Luke omits Peter's rebuke in Mark 8:33.

Purpose of Incomprehension

Beck sees Jesus' impending suffering and death at Jerusalem as being completely incomprehensible to the disciples, and through the journey motif, Luke aimed to show how difficult it was for the disciples to gain insight into Jesus' mission and purpose of coming.[38] Moreover, as Conzelmann suggests, this theme points to the impossibility of knowing the full significance of Jesus' earthly ministry before his death.[39] The theme also serves point to presenting Jesus' instruction to the Lukan community so that they could progress in their understanding of Jesus and his instruction.

Thematic Study of Incomprehension

Nolland sees that Peter's confession at 9:20 provides the foundation from which Jesus can elucidate the Messianic task to which he is committed.[40] While Jesus leads the disciples on the way to Jerusalem, he predicts his upcoming persecution. However, the disciples fail to grasp it (9:44-45; 18:34). Thus, Peter, who stands out as representative of the disciples, becomes impertinent and chiding when Jesus asks, "Who touched me?" (8:42-48). The disciples become perplexed at Jesus' challenge that they feed the crowd in the desert (9:12-13). Made "dull" by heavy sleep, Peter, John, and James experience only part of the revelation on the Mount of Transfiguration and Peter talks without understanding (9:32-33). When they return from the mountain, Jesus recognises that the disciples have failed to avail themselves of his power to heal the demon-possessed boy (9:37-43).

The disciples show themselves to be "status-conscious" (9:46-48; 18:15-17), as they argue about which of them will be the greatest, and likewise, as they try to refuse children access to Jesus. The disciples tried to be exclusive by preventing a "friendly exorcist" from casting out demons in Jesus' name (9:49-50). As the disciples celebrate the power given to them, Jesus cautions them that such a joy is not rightly placed and that the true reason for rejoicing is that their names have been written in the book of life (10:17-20). Similarly, when Jesus speaks about his passion in 9:43-45, the disciples fail to understand (24:25-27, 44-45, 50-53).

Despite the fact that the disciples are given the secrets of God's kingdom (8:9-10), they mistakenly suppose that Jesus' nearness to Jerusalem means that the kingdom of God is about to arrive in splendour (19:11). A reason why Jesus tells the parable of the pounds (19:11-27) is to teach that the disciples' first priority is not to look for the final manifestation of the Kingdom of God but to be faithful in doing the work that Jesus has entrusted to them.

Similarly, in the concluding chapters, Jesus speaks to his disciples in public (20:45-21:4) and explains the nature of discipleship, to which the disciples are called. Then, Jesus moves into an eschatological discourse (21:5-36), where he predicts the events leading up to the end of the age. Through this, Jesus lays up further instruction on discipleship. However, the disciples continue to "misunderstand."

Kingsbury examines "incomprehension" and shows that even until section 22:1-24:53, the disciples continue to show their incomprehension of the plan of salvation and about the events in which they are caught.[41] However, at the end, Jesus enlightens the disciples about the plan of salvation, so that they finally grasp the spiritual significance of Jesus' earthly ministry (24:25-27, 44-45, 50-53).[42]

Lukan Epistemology and the Community

Unlike Mark, Luke softens the distinction between those to whom the secrets have been revealed and those outside, suggesting that the boundaries could be easily crossed.[43] This is perhaps because Luke, even more than Mark and Matthew, places more value on human ability to choose than God's choice.[44] Luke's distinctive view on discipleship emphasises "counting the cost." This suggests that, in a sense, one's eternal destiny comes through counting the cost of following Jesus. This is also clear in the case of the rich young man in Luke 18:22-25 and the rich fool in 12:13-21. The hindrance for both of them was that their faith was in their wealth rather than on Jesus. Thus, Luke lays a greater emphasis on human will in one's coming to Christ.

Commenting on the parable of the sower in 8:1-15, Nolland points to the division that divides humanity into two categories. However, like Beck, he rightly observes that for Luke this division is not to be complacently accepted. Transition may occur from one category to another. This is clear as the whole thrust of the context is towards sowing the seed and causing the light to shine (vv. 16-17).[45] Forbes convincingly quotes Parrot, who holds that parables have repentance as the unifying theme.[46] Thus, Forbes rightly concludes that the parables make an important contribution to the theme of reversal by demonstrating the basis, upon which reversal takes place, which is rejection of Jesus by humankind.[47] He explains it on the basis of the text when he says, "The Samaritan (implicitly) has life because he fulfilled the love command, whereas the religious insiders do not (10:25-37).

"The invited guests exclude themselves on the Great Feast (14:15-24), because they refuse to attend the banquet. The estranged younger son is welcomed and restored on the basis of his turn to the father (15:11-24). The rich man is consigned to torment because he did not repent (16:27-31). The tax-collector's contribution before God resulted in his acceptance, while the self-righteous and exclusive attitude of the Pharisee is condemned (18:9-14)."[48] Kingsbury brings out the above perspective when he says that the disciples' failure rests partly on themselves as well as on divine intention. He further says that whatever the tension between the two parts, each must be given its due.[49] Based on this study, I hold that Luke presents human freedom in the context of God's sovereignty.

Moreover, like Mark, Luke also presents the Jewish Shema as the key to inheriting eternal life (10:25f). However, the incomplete understanding of the legal expert and his willful negligence towards obeying the "Shema" becomes evident in his next question in verse 29. Through this question and Jesus' subsequent response, Luke aimed to emphasise the futility of superficially inquiring from Jesus without accepting him. Since Jesus is God's son, the Shema is now fulfilled through committing oneself to follow Jesus.[50] Nolland explains the greatest commandment as follows:[51]

> Loving God with the heart requires a response to God (Jesus) from the innermost center of our being; loving Him with our life (soul) or the force that energizes us: our consciousness; loving Him with strength, which introduces the action of energetic physical action; And loving with the mind identifies the importance beyond the emotional, of the thinking and planning process, which the mind contributes.

Luke also seems to highlight that not until the disciples understand the saving purposes of God in Jesus, would the disciples be able to undertake the worldwide ministry Jesus has in store for them (24:44-49).[52] Failing this understanding, the disciples would be unproductive in God's kingdom. The community would have known about the vital need to understand and obey Jesus and his teachings.

Conclusion

Luke presents Jesus as God's eschatological "Son of God", who provides a "New Exodus" (salvation) for those who follow him on "the Way." The Gospel was written during that post-Temple destruction period for a mixed community. It strengthened their conviction regarding Jesus and the validity of his promises. It also gave them confidence regarding their participation in his multi-ethnic community. The disciples play an important role in Luke's task. They serve as examples for demonstrating how difficult it is to grasp the mystery of Jesus and his evaluative point of view. The Gospel would have helped the reader to understand the Jewish rejection of Jesus as well as their persecution by the world.

Thus, on the one hand, the above-mentioned point would lead the reader (and hearers) to understand that their ongoing persecution is a result of the incomprehension of their persecutors. On the other hand, it would help the community to continue in understanding the significance of their lives in the light of the larger continuing plan of God through Jesus Christ.

End Notes

[1] Quoted in Moreland, *Love*, 19.

[2] Nolland suggest that Luke and Acts should be studied together as he holds that only the reader who already had Acts in hand will do full justice to the subtle literary foreshadowings which Luke from time to time employs. Thus, Acts (post-Easter) provides a key to understand the Gospel of Luke (John Nolland, *Luke 1 – 9:20*, WBC, vol. 35A (Waco, Texas: Word Books, 1983), xxxiv. See also John Riches, William R. Telford and Christopher M. Tuckett, eds, *The Synoptic Gospels*, Sheffield: Sheffield Press, 2001), 256-57.

[3] D. L. Bock, "Luke, Gospel of," in *DJG*, eds. Joel B. Green and Scott McKnight, (Downers Grove, Ill.: IVP, 1992), 498.

[4] Elsewhere, Bock shows how Luke's emphasis on Gentile inclusion, indicates that the Jesus movement still existed within a Jewish context. D. L. Bock, *Luke*, The IVP New Testament Commentary Series (Leicester: IVP, 1994), 18.

[5] Leonard Doohan, *The Perennial Spirituality* (Santa Fee, New Mexico: Bear & Company, Inc. 1970), 92.

[6] Bock, "Luke, Gospel of," 498.

[7] Forbes, Greg W. *The God of the Old: The Role of the Lukan Parables in the Purpose of Luke's Gospel*, JSNT Suppl. Ser., 198 (Sheffield: Sheffield Press, 2000), 327.

[8] In his major work *Community and the Gospel of Luke,* Esler suggests that the Lukan community was initially closely attached to Judaism, whether as Jews or God fearers; a community that was undergoing persecution. Esler concludes that Luke's story thus provides such a legitimation for the Christian community by providing a symbolic universe and a total world view, to explain and defend the origin of the movement and its separation from its parent body. Philip Francis Esler, *Community and Gospel in Luke-Acts.* SNTS Mon. Ser., 57 (Cambridge: Cambridge University Press, 1996), 65-67.

[9] Bock, *"Luke, Gospel of,"* 498.

[10] Nolland, *Luke 1 – 9:20,* xxxviii.

[11] His Temple loyalty could be seen in the light of his larger agenda to present Jesus as one who truly fulfills the Scriptures (Lk. 24:26-27; 9:31, where the explicit mention of ἔξοδος underlines the idea of a new Exodus for the people of God) and one who is not against the Jewish faith. Tuckett says that in Luke the whole era of Jesus (and the Church) is one of the fulfillment of Jewish hopes and expectations (Tuckett, *The Synoptic,* 281).

[12] Tuckett, *The Synoptic,* 259.

[13] Many detailed changes in Luke from the parallel passages in Mark is easy to envisage if Mark came first, and much harder to envisage in reverse if Mark came last. John Riches, William R. Telford and Christopher M. Tuckett, eds, *The Synoptic,* 263.

[14] Wilkins, *Following,* 209.

[15] Wilkins, *Following,* 209.

[16] This is clear as Luke emphasizes that the fruits must judge the external statements of commitment (6:43-49; 19:11-27). This is possible through one's wholehearted devotion to Jesus.

[17] This is a metaphor used in the early tradition used to denote 'entering into eternal life' (Wilkins, *Following,* 209).

[18] Brian E. Beck, *Christian Character in the Gospel of Luke* (London: Epworth, 1989), 90.

[19] Reminders of journey motif punctuate Luke's central section from 9:51-19:27: 9:51; 10:38; 13:2, 33; 14:25; 17:11; 18:31, 35; 19:1, 11. Through the journey motif, Luke aims to solidify the relation between the disciples and the master and to encourage people to join him on the journey of serving God's purpose. (Joel B. Green, *Theology of Gospel of Luke,* NTT (Cambridge: Cambridge University Press, 1995), 105. The journey motif is especially transparent in 24:13-35, where Jesus meets the two disciples on the road to Emmaus, and instructs them in the Scriptures (24:27). *Ibid.,* 103.

[20] Green, *Theology*, 102. A longest journey is in 9:51-19:27, where Jesus teaches his disciples on the way to Jerusalem. (Green, *Theology*, 103).

[21] Green, 107.

[22] Leonard Doohan, *The Perennial Spirituality* (Santa Fee, New Mexico: Bears and Company Incorporation, 1982), 214.

[23] I. Howard Marshall, *The Gospel of Luke: A Commentary on Greek Text*, NIGTC (Grand Rapids, Michigan: Eerdmans, 1987), 325. He shows how Luke adds pisteuw to his source, thereby showing that the message of Jesus must be heard with faith and the aorist participle indicates an initial faith and the present tense in 8:13 indicates that a continuing attitude is meant. Luke thus implies hearing and doing (6:47).

[24] Nolland, *Luke 1 – 9:20*, 246.

[25] Wilkins, *Following*, 210.

[26] Wilkins, *Following*, 211. This is evident threefold repeated refrain in verses 26, 27 and 33, where Jesus describes the cost of discipleship in terms of allegiances to family, self-will, and one's all (Lk. 14:25-33).

[27] Walter E. Pilgrim, *Good News to the Poor* (Minneapolis: Augsburg Publishing House, 1981), 48.

[28] Beck, *Christian*, 109.

[29] Wilkins, *Following*, 222.

[30] Nolland, *Luke 1 – 9:20*, 486.

[31] Doohan, *Perennial*, 214.

[32] First, it presupposes a radically mixed community in its attention to potentially offensive details about the Law, Table fellowship and other practices (Acts 6:1-6, 10-11, 15). Second, its vigorous defense of the Gentile mission contrasts with the situation in the eighties when the Gentile character of the Christian movement was accepted. Third, it provides believers reassurance in the midst of intense Jewish pressure (Bock, "Luke, Gospel of," 499).

[33] Bock, "Luke, Gospel of," 498.

[34] Hans Conzelmann, *The Theology of St. Luke*, Trans. Geoffrey Buswell (New York: Harper and Row, 1953), 56.

[35] Jack Dean Kingsbury, *Conflict in Luke: Jesus, Authorities, Disciples* (Minneapolis: Fortress Press, 1991), 19. Although Jesus repeatedly tells the disciples about his passion, his predictions are nonetheless hid from them and they receive them 'without understanding' (9:44-45; 18:31-34).

[36] Green, *Theology*, 108.

[37] Conzelmann, *The Theology*, 56.

[38] Beck, *Christian*, 115.

[39] Conzelmann, *The Theology*, 93.

[40] Nolland, *Luke 1 – 9:20*, 452.

[41] *Ibid.*, 127.

[42] *Ibid.*, 127.

[43] Beck, *Christian*, 93.

[44] *Ibid.*, 71.

[45] Nolland, *Luke 1-9:20*, 246.

[46] Parrot demonstrates that pericopae 7:36-50 and 18:9-14 bracket the parables of 'repentance' (Forbes, *The God*, 249).

[47] *Ibid.*, 248.

[48] *Ibid.*, 248.

[49] *Ibid.*, 120.

[50] Greg W. Forbes has argued that through the parables, Luke invites Theophilus (and his extended audience) to compare the views of God held by the opponents of Jesus with the portrait of God presented by Jesus. Forbes, *The God*, 326.

[51] Nolland, *Luke 9:21- 18:34*, WBC, vol. 35B (Waco, Texas: Word Books, 1993), 585.

[52] Kingsbury, *Conflict in Luke*, 110.

CHAPTER 4

The Role of the Mind in Johannine Discipleship

> The God of the Jews was to exist in the Word and through the Word, an unprecedented conception requiring the highest order of abstract thinking.
>
> —Neil Postman[1]

Introduction

In this chapter, we will look at the role of incomprehension or misunderstanding in discipleship in the fourth Gospel. Since context plays a vital role in our present study, we shall therefore examine the original audience, also addressed as the Johannine community.[2] John 21:24 shows that the "beloved disciple" is indirectly responsible for the Gospel.[3] Then we look at the concept of discipleship, which is followed by a brief look at the Wisdom motif, as it stands directly related to our present research. This leads to a discussion on the epistemological framework of this Gospel. Examining the theme of incomprehension follows this topic. In the fourth Gospel, the disciples do not understand or misunderstand Jesus' identity, his words and mission. Finally, the discussion moves to the theme of incomprehension in relation to the Johannine community.

Johannine Community

Moloney holds that we can discern the real readers of the fourth Gospel through the life of the intended reader in the narrative.[4] Thus, we have attempted to trace a picture of the Johannine community based on textual evidence. Brook sees verse 3:21 as part of the evangelist's understanding about the community as the bearer of God's light.[5] Witherington sees this community (of Jewish[6] and Gentile[7] converts) to be settled in Ephesus[8] during the last decade of the first century[9] and one that struggled to maintain relations[10] with their fellow non-believing Jews.[11]

Smalley points to the internal conflict within this community,[12] especially in the realm of Christology.[13] He goes on to say that on the one hand, Jewish Christians struggled to think that Jesus was fully divine; on the other hand, there were Hellenistic-Christians,[14] who tended to see Jesus as less than fully human.[15]

Portrait of Discipleship

Brook, in line with Culpepper[16] and Collins,[17] shows how the absence of any reference to the location of the conversation in 1:35-42 gives the scene a context-free quality that universalises the invitation of Jesus to those who would be his followers (1:43).[18] Wilkins asserts how John's Gospel makes a distinction between true and false disciples based on the types of belief responses.[19]

Moreover, the fourth Gospel stresses that a growing belief is vitally important in discipleship[20] as, in John, belief is not static but continually needs to grow. This is because a continuous knowing and understanding of the Father and the Son is needed to *remain* in the life-giving relationship.[21] Wilkins asserts this point when he says that genuine faith accords with a progressive recognition and understanding of Jesus' true identity and mission.[22] Culpepper also observes how the disciples' ability to continue following Jesus is based on the cognitive perception of the hearers; for example, for some, the words of Jesus are offending (6:60), while for others, they are words of eternal life (6:68).[23]

Pointing to the need of persistence in discipleship, Culpepper, in line with Witherington,[24] sees that John differentiates between the true and false disciples on the basis of a consistent following of Jesus (cf. 8:31).[25] Thus, for John discipleship is possible when one not only makes a believing response to Jesus, but also continues to grow in faith through a progressive and growing understanding of Jesus' identity, instruction and mission.

Jesus as Wisdom Incarnate

In the pre-New Testament era, wisdom was understood to be God's agent in creation.[26] In explaining Jesus as the creative "Logos", the Evangelist asserts the unique function of Jesus, as the one who reveals God (1:18, 17:3). In this way, Jesus performs the role of wisdom.[27] Witherington holds that the "I am" sayings, the miracles and the discourses of Jesus become comprehensible in the light of sapiential literature.[28]

Bennema shows how Jesus in his mission of revealing the Father takes over the picture of wisdom of old. Thus, Jesus in his teaching and instruction, performs the function of wisdom (Pr. 1:23; 13:14; Wisd.7:21; Sir. 4:11; 24:33).[29] Bennema also shows how Jesus' words, such as wisdom instruction, are salvific in that through their acceptance and adherence, one receives life, whereas their rejection leads to death.[30] This presupposes the role of the mind since it requires a person to utilise his or her cognitive abilities to make a positive response to Jesus.

In a similar vein, Jesus is treated as "Light" (in chapters 8 and 9), which brings people out of blindness just as in Solomon's wisdom, where the author sees the pillar of fire as God's means of illuminating the children of Israel, earlier imprisoned in darkness.[31] Thus, Jesus as God's wisdom incarnate brings saving words from the Father and opens the gate to know and understand Him.

Nature of John's Gospel

The prologue's placement at the beginning of the narrative is part of the author's strategy. This prepares the reader to understand the prose narrative of the Gospel (1:19-20:31) in the form of positive and negative human responses.[32] Moloney describes the prologue as follows: In 1:3c-4, the author asserts that the pre-existent Word provided life when it appeared through a historical act that has a continual relevance. This was the light of humankind. Based on verse 5, Moloney says that the author aims to clarify that there was an event in the past where light and darkness clashed, which points to the event of the Cross. However, the light has not been overcome; it still shines. This Moloney sees as the first description of a negative response to the coming of the Word. Although the reader had already been prepared for the theme of rejection of the Word in verse 5, the affirmation in v.10c comes like a shock. Moloney sees this verse as pointing to the evil at large that *will not* accept the revelation brought by the Word.[33]

Regarding the purpose of the Gospel, Witherington exclaims that it was written to the Johannine community as an evangelistic tool that spoke not only about how to become but also about how to remain a Christian.[34] Painter observes quest and rejection stories in the Gospels.[35] In addition to this, Witherington sees the fourth Gospel as having numerous similarities with the later sapiential writings,[36] where God is personified as Wisdom in action.[37] In yet another perspective, Smalley,[38] Culpepper[39] and Moloney[40] see the fourth Gospel as continuous narrative prose that presents Jesus as the Christ, the "Son of God", and calls for faith in Jesus (19:35; 20:31).

Besides the above views, Raymond and D. Moody Smith[41] point to two levels of reading found in this Gospel: Firstly, at the level of narrative tale; and secondly, at a more symbolic level, where it tells the story of the Johannine community in their struggles, particularly about the Jesus enigma.[42] George Beasley-Murray also makes a similar point when he says, "John presents an 'informed vision' of the historical Christ that simultaneously gives an answer to the Christological questions[43] of the time of its composition."[44] Pointing to the strong emphasis on Christology, Smith says that the Fourth Evangelist transposes the apocalyptic hopes and categories of Paul and the other Gospels into another key by subsuming eschatology under Christology.[45] Thus, the Fourth Gospel presents Jesus, as "Son of God" in order to clarify the doubts concerning his identity. It has also developed the theme of "Wisdom" from the sapiential writings, thereby projecting Jesus as the "Wisdom incarnate." Through this, the Fourth Evangelist exhorted his audience to continue progressing in their faith and to also share their faith with others.

Johannine Epistemology

While in Mark no one initially knew Jesus' identity, not even those closest to him, in John, Jesus himself reveals his own identity from the beginning.[46] Moloney contends that John presents Jesus as "God's self-revelation"[47] within the context of the "wayward paths of human freedom."[48] The fourth evangelist operates under a dualistic framework. The dualism is evident from the prologue, where the evangelist utilises the concept of light/darkness and above/below.[49] Kysar sees that this framework is also explained by "truth and falsehood" dualism.[50] Bennema explains this dualism; he shows that humans belong to the earthly realm (3:3; 8:23, 47), due to which they do not possess the necessary epistemic "sight" or understanding required to enter the realm of "above."[51] He calls this human predicament "epistemic darkness."

As stated before, knowing or understanding is inevitable and precedes an adequate believing response.[52] Bennema asserts that a new birth is accomplished by an understanding of Jesus' revelation (3:9-13) facilitated by the cognitive divine agent, the Holy Spirit (6:63).[53] Smith suggests that the message of Jesus was to some extent comprehensible to the disciples, while to others, it was not.[54] Thus, while the disciples at times lacked faith and understanding about Jesus' words, John presents them as those who had sufficiently understood Jesus to make a saving response. By the use of a diagram,[55] Benemma effectively shows how a human being comes to the saving knowledge of Jesus according to John's epistemological understanding.

People's epistemic darkness

Saving truth present in Jesus' revelation

Mediated to people by the Spirit in order to facilitate

Spirit aided human belief

Birth of the Spirit + being in relationship with God

Believer has access to further truth

The Spirit continues as an epistemic agent

Further human belief response and further appropriation of knowledge of the divine

However, a question arises about those (especially among the Jews) who do not make a believing response to Jesus. In this regard, John 12:39-40 and 9:39 seem to suggest that God determines to discloses himself to few "insiders" (disciples) while depriving others "outsiders" (opponents or interlocutors) of light.[56] However, based on 12:39-40, Bennema argues that the fourth Evangelist stresses more on the human initiative in becoming "insiders." He says, "John 12:39-40 refers to the resulting condition and inevitable consequence of rejecting Jesus rather than the result of divine predestination."[57] Similarly, Culpepper says how the dualistic nature[58] of symbols in the Fourth Gospel, more than the Synoptic Gospels, stresses human responsibility to understand these symbols.[59]

Moloney also points to the importance of human initiative when he shows how the negative form of the verb ginoskw in the Fourth Gospel indicates a willful refusal on the part of the hostile world to accept the revelation brought by the Word (5:40; 8:27 cf. 8: 43, 55; 10:38; 16:8-9; 17:23, 25a).[60] Bennema sees precisely this closed-mindedness of some, as a state of "epistemic blindness" that prevents them from knowing God.[61] Commenting on 3:19, Brook says that in John, judgment is a matter of freely chosen attitude and behavior,[62] particularly of the sin of unbelief (Jn. 16:8-9).[63] Pointing to the complexity involved in a person's coming to Jesus, Ridderbos, along with Moloney[64] and Kysar,[65] rightly explains this as Jesus' call to humans for doing what they cannot do by themselves.[66] This is just as a lame man is told to arise and the dead to become alive again. Thus, Bennema rightly says that John's epistemology is principally a Pneumatological (Spirit-informed) and Christocentric epistemology.[67]

In line with his view of kosmoj,[68] the fourth evangelist describes Satan as the "ruler of this world" (12:31; 14:60; 16:11), "the Father of lies" and thereby father of all liars, through which he is involved in carrying out his plans of opposing the Truth (8:44).

Besides this picture of Satan, the Fourth Gospel does not emphasise upon the evil activity as the cause behind keeping people from understanding Jesus and his teachings.[69] Rather, as Kysar in agreement with Bennema[70] rightly says, "this Gospel is more concerned to show how humans have been deformed by misunderstanding and avoids the temptation to abdicate responsibility and to attribute faithlessness to cosmic evil."[71]

John also impresses upon the readers that though there was enough revelation for making a saving response to Jesus, understanding about the identity and mission of Jesus in the manner of post-Easter understanding, was not possible before the "Cross." This is because Jesus' distinctive role in John as the one who reveals the Father and authenticates the children of God culminates at the Cross.[72] Smith in line with Thompson[73] argues for the above point and views Jesus' death as the hour of his glorification[74] (Jn.7: 39; 12:16; 12:23; 13:31) and highest point of self-revelation.[75] This is also clear, as unlike Mark, in John the "hour" always refers to Jesus' death and subsequent glorification. In this way, John narrates the whole ministry of Jesus from the perspective of Jesus' death.[76] Regarding Jesus' death Smith succinctly says, "Jesus' death is the crucial moment of God's self-revelation and judgment. It opens the way to the future as the time of the risen and ascended Christ (cf. 20:17) and of the Spirit-Paraclete who continues and extends his revelation."[77]

The preceding discussion shows that, in John, salvation is a result of understanding followed by a believing response to God's self-revelation in Jesus. Such a response is facilitated by the help of the Holy Spirit, who acts as an epistemic agent.[78] So, as Benemma rightly explains, for John, knowledge-belief is one salvific package, in that a saving belief requires or contains a certain adequate degree of knowledge of the divine.[79]

While the powers of darkness are active, they are not ultimately responsible for blinding the "outsiders." Rather, it is their own unbelieving mind that hinders them from experiencing the eternal life in Jesus. However, as Witherington and others[80] have pointed out, in John, knowledge of the *full* mystery of who Jesus is, was not possible before the crucifixion, resurrection and before the Spirit bestowal by Jesus.[81]

Theme of Incomprehension

There is evidence of the disciples' incomprehension[82] and misunderstanding[83] during Jesus' ministry. In this sense, though the disciples are like others, yet they do not come under judgment, because while the former respond with hostility and unbelief, the latter respond with perplexity. Bennema sees the cause of the disciples' continued struggles in their understanding, as the result of "epistemic cloudiness" that remains for the "insiders."[84] This "cloudiness" is the reason for the disciples' struggle to grasp the things "from above." However, Culpepper argues that the cause behind the disciples' incomprehension was partly from the necessity that their faith be incomplete until the Cross. This again affirms the importance of the death of Jesus for a full understanding of Jesus and his purpose.[85]

This state of epistemic cloudiness continues to effect the believers even after the Cross event. The Fourth Evangelist also highlights the ministry of the Holy Spirit that causes the disciples to gradually grow in their understanding of Jesus and his mission. Regarding this, Thompson rightly says that after Jesus' resurrection, the Paraclete assumes the role of a teacher (16:13), guiding the disciples into all truth, reminding them of Jesus' words.[86]

Purpose of Incomprehension

Pointing to the effect of the disciples' inaptitude for the Johannine community, Moloney sees the various misunderstandings of the disciples (e.g. 1:38; 2:19-20; 3:3-4; 4:10-11; 6:32-34; 18:37-38), as summons to the readers to make a decision about Jesus Christ.[87] Culpepper sees all the misunderstandings in John as a result of ambiguous statements.[88] He observes the brain-teasing nature of the symbols, whose repeated use incites the sensitive readers to grasp the knowledge of the "higher level" with increasing appreciation.[89] In this sense, the symbols act as bridges by which the reader *may* cross in some elusive sense into the reality and mystery, the life, which they represent.[90] Painter argues that "misunderstanding" and "incomprehension" clarify Jesus' identity and viewpoint.[91] Thus, misunderstanding acts as an avenue for a deeper insight into the Evangelist's thought world.[92] It also leads the audience with the Evangelist to a shared perception of meaning and reverence before the enigma of the risen Christ.[93]

Collins presents a negative function of "misunderstanding" when he says, "throughout John's gospel 'misunderstandings' are used as a literary device to describe inadequate faith that does not lead to salvation." Collins portrays Nicodemus as a first example of one who serves as an example that John uses to present the meaning of authentic faith in Jesus."[94] Through this, the Evangelist shows the serious consequences of misunderstanding.[95] Thus, the misunderstandings and incomprehension call upon the readers to make efforts to understand the words of Jesus in order to make an adequate faith response.

Thematic Study of Incomprehension

The Gospel begins with Jesus as the key to the mystery of God, which stands behind the story.[96] The Fourth Evangelist presents evidence of the disciples' misunderstanding and incomprehension and shows how the disciples initially did not grasp the meaning of Jesus' ministry (Jn. 2:21-22; 4:27, 33; 6:60; 9:2; 10:6; 11:8, 11-15; 12:16; 13:36; 14:5,8,22; 16:17-18). However, he goes further to show how the disciples make their way to comprehend Jesus' full status as the "Son of God."

Smith shows how in John 1:51, Jesus utters a rather enigmatic suggestion of what the disciples may expect to witness during his ministry.[97] Culpepper observes the Johannine plot is propelled by conflict between believing and unbelieving responses to Jesus.[98] During Jesus' earthly ministry recorded in John 2-11, while Jesus does not directly teach the disciples, his public words are equally relevant for them as it is for his opponents.[99] Thus, when Jesus' interlocutors opposed him, the disciples sought to understand and follow Jesus.

Regarding chapters 2-12, Smith rightly points out that while almost all monologues of Jesus invariably lead to some hostile rejection (Jn. 6:2, 24-26, 41, 60, 66; 12:37; and 13:27-30), the Evangelist often goes out of his way to note that some believe (Jn. 6:68-69; 7:40-41).[100] Similarly, regarding the private discourse in chapters 13-17, Moloney shows that the profound teaching, especially in the discourses of Jesus, is not so much an explanation of the fundamentals beliefs as an exhortation to understand and apply that belief.[101] Thus, through the theme of "incomprehension", John shows the need to understand Jesus' identity and his teachings in order to make an adequate saving response and to sustain discipleship.[102]

Johannine Epistemology and the Church

Smith sees that the words of Jesus (5:47) that reveal the meaning of his coming and deeds are, at their very best, retrospective, that is, one could have not have known them prior to Jesus' death and resurrection.[103] Similarly, Witherington argues that the author has a firm grasp on historical distinctions, particularly in regard to the disciples' knowledge before and after Easter.[104] Thus, the Evangelist shows that the disciple had not fully understood the identity and mission of Jesus before Easter.[105] However, even after Easter, disciples like Thomas doubted them. It is precisely in this context that the events of 20:30-31 take place. Smalley rightly argues that, through the episode of Thomas, John exhorts his readers to continue believing in Jesus.[106]

Moloney says that, through the Prologue, the author has communicated to the readers with exalted notions about Jesus Christ, which are to be tested by the story of his life.[107] Since, understanding is an index to "outsiders" and "insiders", John exhorts his multi-ethnic Johannine community to understand Jesus aright in order to grow in discipleship.

Conclusion

The Gospel presents Jesus as God's self-revelation to humankind whose existence had been devoid of God's knowledge. This Gospel was written to a community of believers who were undergoing rejection and persecution because of their faith in Jesus. Various heretical groups that aimed to undermine the Christological significance of Jesus also surrounded the community. There are suggestions that the community was also undergoing internal Christological conflict. Thus, the Gospel seeks to present Jesus as fully human and fully divine; the one who revealed the Father to the darkened human race. Jesus' sacrifice on the Cross reveals the Father. Moreover, after Jesus' death, he does not leave the disciples alone, but gives them the helper, the Holy Spirit, who guides them in ways of Truth.

In the Gospel presentation, the disciples stand out as important characters. While they confessed Jesus as the "Messiah" right at the beginning of the Gospel narrative, they were unable to understand completely the identity and mission of Jesus till the latter part of Jesus' ministry (16:30-31). In this respect, they were just like the crowds and the Jewish opponents. Yet, they were different from them in that they responded to Jesus with a saving belief. Thus, even in their failures and inaptitude, they stand as positive examples for the community to emulate. At the same time, their lives also suggest the difficulty of understanding Jesus and his mission even when they were recipients of Jesus' private instruction.

Through the Gospel, the community and the prospective readers are, thus, presented with a detailed eyewitness account of Jesus' life and ministry. Through the disciples' lives and other characters, the community was thus encouraged to understand Jesus aright and to persevere in the path of discipleship. This discipleship, as John suggests, is possible only through a growing perception about Jesus and his continued purposes as he reveals them each day through the help of the Holy Spirit.

End Notes

[1] Quoted in Moreland, *Love*, 19

[2] Regarding this, Culpepper says that the Gospel was shaped by the life of the community. (R. Alan Culpepper, *The Gospel and the Letters of John*, Interpreting Biblical Texts Series (Nashville: Abingdon, 1998), 42.

[3] Thompson, "John, Gospel of," 370. See also Wes Howard Brook, *Becoming Children of God: John's Gospel and Radical Discipleship* (New York: Orbis, 1994), 15. Regarding the date of writing, Thompson bases his view upon the section of the Gospel (18:31-33) found in Rylands Papyrus 457 P57 dating early Second century CE, which suggests that John cannot have been published later than the end of the first century or very early in the second. (Thompson, "John, Gospel of," 370.)

[4] Francis J. Moloney, *Belief in the Word: John 1-4* (Minneapolis: Fortress Press, 1998), 14.

[5] Brook, *Becoming*, 93. He sees the 'we' in 3:11 as also pointing to prologue (1:11-12) that puts the Johannine community in the same position as the light. (Brook, *Becoming*, 90.)

[6] The Scripture fulfillment theme (12:14-15, 37-41; 19:24, 28, 36-37) suggests that there were at least some of Jewish extraction in the target audience. Ben Witherington III, *John's Wisdom: A Commentary on the Fourth Gospel* (Louisville, Kentucky: Westminster John Knox Press, 1995), 34.

[7] Brook sees a chiastic pattern in 1:38-1:42. Since John translates Hebrew words at three occasions in this small chiasm, it provides the social implication that at least some of the audience was not Jewish, or at least not Hebrew. He also has shown how the text oscillates between the audience's familiarity with Jewish things (e.g. 2:13; 7:2; 13:1) and in providing detailed explanation (e.g. 4:9). This suggests that at best, John's community was a mixed community. (Brook, *Becoming*, 71.) Thus, in Jn. 12:32, where Jesus is the Savior of the world who draws 'all people' unto himself (see also, 1:29; 3:17; 4:42). Stephen S. Smalley, *John Evangelist and Interpreter* (Illinois: IVP, 1998), 181.

[8] Witherington, *John's Wisdom: A Commentary on the Fourth Gospel* (Louisville, Kentucky: Westminster John Knox Press, 1995), 29. He asserts this on the basis of the following points: (a) there is considerable testimony to the Beloved Disciple being in Ephesus in Asia until the end of his life, in Irenaeus, and elsewhere; (b) the 'evqhnoj' of the Fourth Gospel suggests a place that is predominantly Gentile in character, but which nonetheless has a strong Jewish presence, Witherington, *John's*, 29. Painter and Beasley-Murray also make a similar point. John Painter, *The Quest for the Messiah: The History, Literature and Theology of Johannine Community* (Edinburgh: T&T Clark, 1991), 19; and George R. Beasley-Murray, "Enigma of the Gospel," in WBC, ed. Bruce M. Metzger, vol. 36. CD ROM. (accessed on November 05, 2004).

[9] Witherington, *John's Wisdom*, 38. Witherington sees this period when polemical shots are being fired at each other from two already distinguishable groups of Johannine community and Synagogue, Witherington, Ibid., 39. In similar lines, Ridderbos sees the Gospel as a product of advanced theology about Jesus in Johannine community. Herman Ridderbos, *The Gospel of John: A Theological Commentary* (Grand Rapids, Michigan: Eerdmans, 1987), 672. Painter also points to the hostility of the Jewish world to the disciples of Jesus as the most important context of the formation it this Gospel. Painter, *Quest for the Messiah*, 24.

[10] Painter in line with Moloney (Moloney, *Belief in the Word*, 14.) builds his case on John 9 and says that in John the tradition portraying Jesus' conflict with Jewish authorities is used in a way that takes account of the conflict experienced by the Johannine community, culminating in their expulsion from the Synagogue. Painter, *Quest for the Messiah*, 8. See also (9:22; 12:42; 16:2); Moloney, *Belief in the Word*, 14. and Robert

Kysar, *John: The Maverick Gospel*, rev. ed. (Louisville, Kentucky: Westminster. 1993), 75.

[11] McGrath suggests that John's Gospel is an attempt of Jewish Christianity (or one strand thereof) to defend itself over against one or more other forms of Judaism. James F. McGrath, *John's Apologetic Christology*, SNTS Mon. Ser., 111 (Cambridge: Cambridge University Press, 2001), 38. See also George R. Beasley-Murray, *John*, WBC, vol. 36 (Waco: Word Books, 1987), xxxiv.

[12] Smalley bases this argument on the Johannine emphasis on mutual love in 15:12 and unity within the church (17:11,21-23). (Smalley, *John Evangelist*, 184.)

[13] Ibid.

[14] Who were still inclined towards their pagan religious background, Ibid.

[15] Ibid.

[16] Culpepper, *Anatomy*, 116.

[17] Raymond F. Collins, *These Things Have Been Written: Studies on the Fourth Gospel* (Grand Rapids, Michigan: Eerdmans, 1990), 48.

[18] Brook, *Becoming*, 71. While the disciples ask about where Jesus abides, he calls them to 'come and see'. Thus, in following him, the disciples will see his glory, and in seeing him they will see the Father (2:11; 14:9).

[19] Michael J. Wilkins, *Following the Master: Discipleship in the Steps of Jesus* (Grand Rapids, Michigan: Zondervan, 1992), 226.

[20] Wilkins, *Following*, 228.

[21] Cornelis Bennema, *The Power of Saving Wisdom: An Investigation of Spirit and   Wisdom in Relation to the Soteriology of the Fourth Gospel* (Tübingen: Mohr Siebeck, 2002), 128. This as Bennema rightly points out, is perhaps indicated by the Aorist and present subjunctive of ginwskw in 10:38 (cf. 15:7; 17:3; 20:31).

[22] Wilkins, *Following*, 227.

[23] Culpepper, *Anatomy*, 116.

[24] Witherington, *John's Wisdom*, 176.

[25] Culpepper, *Anatomy*, 116. He shows how the true disciples remember what Jesus said (2:22).

[26] E.g., see Pr. 8:22-30.

[27] Culpepper, *Gospel and Letters of John*, 17 Similarly, based on 3:13, Brook says that the fourth evangelist has used the image from Wisdom tradition to depict Jesus as 'Wisdom Incarnate'. (Brook, *Becoming*, 91.) It is precisely for this reason that Jesus is able to exercise power over natural elements. Also Bennema, *Power*, 157.

[28] Witherington, *John's Wisdom*, 23. This type of literature reflects ways of speaking found in Jewish Wisdom literature. Witherington, *John's Wisdom*, 18. Witherington shows that the Wisdom of Solomon is attributed to the Wisdom of God and God's personified Word is attributed to Jesus, e.g. water from rock in the desert is attributed to Jesus in Jn. 11:1-4. Witherington, *John's Wisdom*, 24.

[29] Bennema, *Power*, 123.

[30] Bennema, *Power*, 123.

[31] Witherington, *John's Wisdom*, 24. Another similarity between John's Gospel and the late Sapiential literature is the incidence of Father and Father-Son language, which is not characteristic of the OT naming of God. In the OT, God is called 'Father' no less that 115 times compared to only five times in Mark and fifteen times in Matthew. Witherington, *John's Wisdom*, 24.

[32] Cornelis Bennema, "What has Athens to Do with Jerusalem? A Study of Johannine Epistemology," in *Bible and Epistemology*, eds. R. Perry and M. Healy (Carlislie: Paternoster, forthcoming 2006), Chapter 7. See also (Thompson, "John, Gospel of," 373.) and (Culpepper, *Anatomy*, 98.)

[33] Moloney, *Belief in the Word*, 24-37.

[34] Witherington, *John's Wisdom*, 32.

[35] Painter, *Quest for the Messiah*, 6.

[36] See Wisd. 7:14ff, where wisdom is said to be the one whose, coming down from above, passes into human souls, renewing all things, and makes them friends of God.

[37] Witherington, *John's Wisdom*, 25.

[38] Smalley, *John Evangelist*, 142.

[39] Culpepper, *Gospel*, 14.

[40] Moloney, *Belief in the Word*, 4.

[41] D. Moody Smith, *Theology of Gospel of John*, NTT (Cambridge: Cambridge University Press, 1995), 102.

[42] Collins, *These Things*, 49.

[43] Painter also sees the primary purpose is to convince that Jesus is the Christ. (Painter, *Quest*, 9.)

[44] Beasley-Murray, "Enigma of the Gospel," in WBC, ed. Bruce M. Metzger, vol. 36. CD ROM. (accessed on November 05, 2004)

[45] Smith, *Theology*, 106. This is because the decisive, eschatological event, the coming of Jesus, has already occurred. In other words, the eschatology is already defined in the light of the coming of Jesus.

[46] Culpepper, *The Gospel*, 15. E.g., 4:26; 9:37; 18:37.

[47] The Gospel presents Jesus in such a way that seeing him is to have seen the Father (12:45; 14:7-9), or to know and receive him is to have known and received the Father (8:19; 12:44; 13:20; 17:8; cf. 15:23). Thompson, "John, Gospel of," 379.

[48] Moloney, *Belief in the Word*, 24. The fourth evangelist uses an emphatic pronoun (ekeinoj) to claim that there is only one who has made God known (v.18c); Jesus who lives in enduring intimate union with the Father. Ibid., 48.

[49] Bennema, "Athens," chapter 7.

[50] For a detailed study see, Robert Kysar, *John: The Maverick Gospel,* rev. ed. (Louisville, Kentucky:Westminster, 1993), 60-66. Smith adds that the sharp dualism of the Gospel should not lead the reader to infer that people immediately fall into two well-defined camps of faith and unbelief. Smith, *Theology,* 110.

[51] Bennema, "Athens," chapter 7.

[52] E.g., in 6:60-66, because of lack of understanding and cognitive inability, people are not able to make an adequate belief-response to Jesus. Bennema shows how 17:3 portrays eternal life as a result of knowing/understanding Jesus and his words, Bennema, "Athens," Chapter 7. Witherington makes a similar point, when he says that knowing the divine plan of revelation and salvation in Jesus makes a person free (from the sphere of darkness), Witherington, *John's Wisdom,* 176-77. Thompson also makes a similar point. See Thompson, "John, Gospel of," 380.

[53] The disciples had already encountered Spirit-Paraclete in Jesus' words, John 6:63 cf. 14:17. Bennema, "Athens," Chapter 7, Section – Human Response and Further Divine Help. Bennema also argues in this way as, pisteuw is based in ginowoskw/oida and integrates the content of ginowoskw/oida. Bennema, *Power,* 133.

[54] Smith, *Theology,* 114.

[55] Cornelis Bennema, 'Christ, the Spirit and the Knowledge of God: A Study in Johannine Epistemology' in M. Healy and R. Parry (eds.), The Bible and Epistemology: Biblical Soundings on the Knowledge of God (Milton Keynes: Paternoster, 2007), 126.

[56] See also 15:16 and 17:6.

[57] Bennema, "Athens," chapter 7, section-'Epistemic Darkness and Illuminating Revelation'.

[58] I.e., their understanding stand as an index to the position of each and every human, i.e. whether they are 'insiders' or 'outsiders'. Culpepper, *Anatomy,* 200.

59 Culpepper, *Anatomy*, 201. See 14:23. Here, one of the disciples ask as why Jesus wants to show himself to the disciples and not to the world. At this point, Jesus' answers implies that human openness and reception of Jesus is the basis of experiencing God's presence.

60 Moloney, *Belief in the Word*, 38. Similarly, the author also uses the negative form of 'oidamen' simply to show that lack of knowledge is the result of human ignorance (see 1:26; 7:28; 8:14, 19; 9:29; 15:21) Ibid., 38.

61 Bennema, "Athens," Chapter 7, Section Epistemic Darkness and Epistemic Darkness.

62 Brook, *Becoming*, 92.

63 Bennema, "Athens," chapter 7- Section 'Epistemic Darkness and Illuminating Revelation.

64 Moloney, *Belief in the Word*, 39.

65 Kysar, *John: The Maverick Gospel*, 72.

66 Ridderbos, *The Gospel of John*, 233.

67 Bennema, "Athens," Chapter 7, Section – Human Response and Further Divine Help.

68 As a realm of darkness, evil and unbelief. Kysar, *John: The Maverick Gospel*, 66.

69 This is also why the fourth Gospel is remarkably silent about the demons. Kysar, *John: The Maverick Gospel*, 67.

70 Bennema observes that in addition to the theme of 'epistemic darkness', 'epistemic blindness' (12:39-40) and particularly sin, which is 'unbelief', that keeps people from knowing God. He does not present 'evil' as the reason that prevents people from the kingdom. Bennema, "Athens,"

Chapter 7.

71 Kysar, *John: The Maverick Gospel*, 67.

72 Culpepper, *Anatomy*, 88.

73 Thompson, "John, Gospel of," 378.

74 Glory is an eschatological term in the New Testament. Smith, *Theology*, 119.

75 Smith, *Theology*, 119.

76 Ibid., 120.

77 Ibid., 120. In this way John's description of Jesus' death as exaltation and glorification is a way of understanding its revelatory character. Ibid, 121.

78 Bennema, *Power*, 129.

[79] Cornelis Bennema, 'Christ, the Spirit and the Knowledge of God: A Study in Johannine Epistemology' in M. Healy and R. Parry (eds.), *The Bible and Epistemology: Biblical Soundings on the Knowledge of God* (Milton Keynes: Paternoster, 2007), 127

[80] Smith, *Theology*, 09; Wilkins, *Following*, 227. and Beasley-Murray, "Enigma of the Gospel."

[81] Witherington, *John's Wisdom*, 176.

[82] See 2:22; 6:60; 10:6; 12:16; 16:17; 20:9 – post-resurrection.

[83] While the disciple(s) call Jesus Messiah (1:41), they do not understand him till 16:30. See also 4:27, 33; 6:7, 19; 9:2; 11:8, 12, (23-24-Martha); 13:36; 14:5; 14:8-9; 24:25b.

[84] Bennema, "Athens," Section- 'Epistemic Darkness and Illuminating Response'.

[85] Culpepper, *Anatomy*, 91. E.g. 2:12 "..they remembered what Jesus said and understood after the resurrection."; 10:16 "..the disciples failed to understand..."; 20:9 "did not yet understand the Scripture that he must rise..."

[86] Thompson, "John, Gospel of," 382.

[87] Moloney, *Belief in the Word*, 12.

[88] Culpepper, *Anatomy*, 160.

[89] Culpepper, *Anatomy*, 201.

[90] Culpepper, *Anatomy*, 201.

[91] Painter, *Quest for the Messiah*, 197.

[92] Smalley, *John Evangelist*, 124.

[93] Culpepper, *Anatomy*, 202.

[94] Collins, *These Things*, 66.

[95] Culpepper, *Anatomy*, 165.

[96] Moloney, *Belief in the Word*, 12.

[97] Smith, *Theology*, 24.

[98] Culpepper, *Anatomy*, 97. He substantiates this position by the fact that almost half of the occurrences of the word "believe" in the New Testament are found in John (98 out of 239). Culpepper, *Anatomy*, 97.

[99] Smith, *Theology*, 111. E.g. In chapter 6, while the bread of heaven discourse is given before the Jews, the disciples are embedded in the discourse.

[100] Ibid., 110.

[101] Smalley, *John Evangelist*, 181.

[102] Bennema, *Power*, 143.

[103] Smith, *Theology*, 113.

[104] Witherington, *John's Wisdom*, 35.

[105] However, as we have argued earlier, the disciples had adequately understood Jesus to make a saving belief response.

[106] Smalley, *John Evangelist*, 175.

[107] Moloney, *Belief in the Word*, 52.

CHAPTER 5

Capturing the Quintessence

We live in what may be the most anti-intellectual period in the history...We must have passion – indeed hearts on fire for the things of God. But that passion must resist with intensity the anti-intellectual spirit of the world.

- R. C. Sproul[1]

Gospel According to St. Mark

Mark presents the life of the Jesus Christ as the "Son of God", who is God's self-revelation to the world. The miracles, as they occur in Mark, present Jesus' real identity. However, not everyone is able to understand him completely even after the miracles. Mark presents the disciples as those who failed time and again to understand Jesus' identity and entered into arguments with Jesus, as they were hard hearted and inept. While the powers of darkness do play a role in confounding humans to remain in the dark, Mark emphasises that it is primarily because of the disciples' (human) dullness and ineptitude to understand the identity (and mission) of Jesus. This is why Peter rebukes Jesus and the disciples show their incomprehension and lack of servant spirit.

Nevertheless, the disciples were not condemned as "outsiders" because they showed their genuine commitment to understand and obey Jesus. This is why, unlike the crowd that followed Jesus only for a short time, the disciples continued to follow Jesus even without full understanding. In their incomprehension, the disciples represent the frustration of Mark's audiences at trying to make sense of Jesus' identity. Throughout Mark's Gospel, the purpose behind the incomprehension of the disciples is to make a point about Jesus' identity. Through this, Mark aims to challenge the readers to appreciate Jesus more through applying their cognitive abilities.

Mark shows the "Cross" as an important point of God's self-revelation. However, the paradoxical "hiddenness" of God's revelation continues to be at work among the believers (and o among the unbelievers). Through this, Mark presents the human difficulty to understand Jesus. Therefore, Mark shows the need to apply the disciples' cognitive abilities as crucial for discipleship. As the community engages itself to understand and know about Jesus, they would also be able to understand the reason why people reject Jesus. Mark aims to illustrate, through the disciples' example, the challenge of understanding Jesus as the Lord and of continually following him with an open mind (as opposed to hard-heartedness) and a learning spirit.

Gospel According to St. Matthew

The Evangelist writes probably to a Christian community closely related to and in opposition with the Jewish synagogue, from which it had recently parted. He presents Jesus as the promised Messiah, the "Son of God", who truly fulfills the Torah and teaches the way of the Lord. He is also "Wisdom incarnate", so that following him amounts to following God. The disciples are those who understand this truth and have committed themselves to follow God, as Jesus reveals Him through his life and teachings.

However, in the process of learning Jesus' instruction, the disciples still fail to understand part of Jesus' words. Based on the parable of the sower, the Evangelist points to the evil powers as only one of the reasons behind people' incomprehension. The Evangelist sees humans as primarily responsible for their incomprehension or misunderstanding. This is clear as he exhorts his hearers to learn from Jesus and make an appropriate response to Jesus.

The Evangelist uses the disciples' incomprehension to mediate "insight" about Jesus' instructions to his community. This implies that Matthew emphasises upon the need for continual engagement of our minds in order to understand and obey Jesus' instructions.

Thus, Matthew exhorted his community and all the readers down through the ages to continue to apply their minds to understand Jesus' instructions in order to bear fruit for the kingdom of God (13:19a), as it depends upon true (and a progressive) understanding. Thus, if one needs to make progress in discipleship, they are to make efforts to understanding Jesus' instructions with an attitude to obey them subsequently.

Gospel According to St. Luke

Luke writes to possibly a mixed community that was undergoing persecution, with an aim to consolidate their faith in Jesus. For Luke, Jesus is the promised Messiah, who fulfills the Scriptures. Therefore, following him is to follow "the Way" of the Lord. Luke develops on the Exodus motif and sees that God provides the true deliverance (complete Exodus) in Jesus. Luke develops the "Exodus" motif through Jesus' journey to Jerusalem, where Jesus' ultimate glory is revealed. For Luke, discipleship does not only involve understanding Jesus' instruction but also obeying them.

The Cross is significant as it provides scope of fuller understanding to the disciples about the passion and the true identity of Jesus. For Luke, one of the reasons for the disciples' misunderstanding and incomprehension is that the resurrection had not yet taken place. It was only after the disciples meet Jesus on the road to Emmaus that he enables them to understand about his passion, which helped them to adequately understand about God's plan of salvation in and through the passion of Jesus Christ. Thus, for Luke, the Cross acts as the turning point to knowing the fuller identity and mission of Jesus.

In addition to this, Luke also points to the human difficulty of comprehending the identity and mission of Jesus. It is precisely because of this reason that the disciples (in the post-resurrection era) are called to make disciplined efforts to understand Jesus' identity and his mission (and also their). In this way, Luke emphasised on the need to understand Jesus and his mission for living meaningful and significant lives as disciples.

Unlike the Pharisees and Jesus' opponents, the disciples are characterised with a willing and an open disposition. The true disciples are those who assess the cost of following Jesus every day. It must be remembered that after one has counted the cost of following Jesus, she or he must make a decision, as no one just flows into discipleship. Through this, Luke also emphasises the need for obedience in discipleship, as this proves true discipleship and true understanding.

Gospel According to St. John

John presents Jesus as the promised Son of God, who truly fulfills the Torah. He writes to a community that was undergoing confusion regarding their view of Jesus in the context of opposing Christological claims. John presents Jesus as God's self-revelation. He is also "Wisdom incarnate", who reveals God's way of salvation. The true disciples are those who understand Jesus and his instructions. Jesus' interlocutors also seem to understand Jesus' instruction, but they willfully reject them. While the disciples understand Jesus' point of view, frequently they also misunderstand or fail to understand. In spite of this, unlike the crowds, the disciples, continued to follow Jesus with a willing and open mind.

The fourth Evangelist presents "the Cross" as the high point of Jesus' self-revelation as "Son of God." Thus, the disciples' misunderstanding and incomprehension was to assert the impossibility of *complete* understanding of Jesus and his purpose before the Cross. However, this does not mean that an adequate understanding to make a saving response was impossible before the Cross. In spite of the strong dualistic framework of the Gospel, the Fourth Evangelist points to the human responsibility to understand Jesus aright in order to make a proper response to Jesus.

The disciples' misunderstanding stands as the evangelists' opportunity to present Jesus' teachings. It also stands to underscore the human difficulty in understanding Jesus' identity and instructions. This difficulty is because of the epistemic cloudiness that continues to envelop the disciples even after the Cross. In this way, the fourth Evangelist encouraged the readers to continually apply their minds to understand and follow the exalted Jesus, who continues to be with his people through the Holy Spirit.

Post-Easter Disciples

Today, we, like the early disciples, are called to be with the exalted Jesus and learn from him the art of living. This is vital and painstaking, as Jesus does not call people to repeat him merely in externals, but to be influenced by him in their deepest, innermost being. This is because while the secrets of God's kingdom have been "revealed", they need to be "unlocked." The teachings of Jesus in the Gospels show us how to live the life we have been given through the time, place, family, neighbour, talents and opportunities that are ours. In this sense, God calls us to do our everyday affairs as Jesus himself would do it. In other words, Jesus' basic message is "rethink your life in the light of the fact that the kingdom of heaven is now open to all" (4:17). It is in this kind of approach that we begin to use our minds to apply the life and teachings of Jesus in everyday life so that we manifest the presence of the kingdom of God in our lives.

In John 8:31-32, Jesus says that we will be liberated from all the bondage that is in human life through sin by continuing in the truth. This reminds us of the need for constantly applying our minds to orient ourselves according to the principles of the Kingdom of God.

Similarly, we are called to be watchful and identify those who would mislead the sheep (as in Matthew 7:15, pointing to the disciples) by observing their word and deeds. This is possible only when we continue to apply our cognitive abilities to discern the difference between the right and the wrong way of understanding Jesus and his instruction (recorded in the Holy Bible). However, this approach should not be seen as just doctrinal correctness. This is because all that we know becomes significant only when the central point of reference is always a divine love and devotion to God. Thus, it is only by being motivated with God's love that one can be truly involved in the eternal quest of knowing and differentiating the right from the wrong way of understanding the truth about Jesus. This would also prevent us from being puffed up or assuming a "holier than thou" attitude in our journey as disciples of Lord Jesus Christ.

Based on our investigation about the role of the cognitive function of the mind in discipleship in the Gospels, we have found that all the four Evangelists presented discipleship in relation to the theme of "incomprehension." They see the Cross as a crucial point of God's self-revelation. Though all four Evangelists operate under a dualistic framework, they go on to emphasise the human responsibility to understand God's revelation given in and through Jesus Christ.

The "Cross" event enabled the disciples to better understand all that Jesus did and said during his earthly life and ministry. Acquiring this understanding was not meant to be static. Rather, it beckoned the disciples to a still deeper engagement of their cognitive abilities to understand the person of Jesus and the mysteries of the kingdom as Jesus led his disciples as the exalted Messiah. In a similar manner, this understanding prompts us to use our cognitive ability in following Jesus.

End Notes

[1] Quoted in J. P. Moreland, *Love Your God With All Your Mind: The Role of Reason in the life of the Soul*, Colorado, Colorado Springs: Navpress, 1997, 19.

CHAPTER 6
Does It Really Matter?

In the preface, we came across Immanuel Kant's three questions that are important for a well-examined life. Let us try to answer these questions on the basis of the insights offered by the Gospel writers. In this book, we have seen how the Gospel writers portray Jesus as God's revelation to the world. Therefore, in response to Kant's first question about what one needs to know, the Gospel writers call us to know the truth about Jesus. The truth is, therefore, not in abstraction, but is anchored in the person of Jesus Christ. All other forms of understanding come from the understanding of this ultimate "truth." He gives the paradigm for life that adds "life" to ordinary human lives and makes life worth living. Responding to Kant's second question about how one decides what is right and what is wrong, the Gospel writers affirm the words of Jesus as presenting the required paradigm.

However, like Pilate, some turn their backs to Jesus and, therefore, deprive themselves from understanding this "truth" in their lives. Pilate had come so close in his conversation with Jesus that he asked him about what truth was. However, it is sad that he did stay on to listen to Jesus but moved away without receiving an answer. I remember what God spoke through his prophet Jeremiah regarding the manner of seeking. It is written, "And you will seek me and find me, when you search for me with *all your heart* (Jer. 29:13)." In a similar fashion, Jesus called people to seek, knock and ask, for those who seek will find, and the door would open to those who knock and those who ask would receive (Mt. 7:7-8). I guess if Pilate had waited for an answer, Jesus would have replied in a manner similar to the one in which he replied to his disciple Thomas: "I am the way, the truth and the life. No one comes to the Father except through Me (Jn. 14:6)." Responding to Kant's third question about what one should be living for, the Gospel writers exhort us to live for Jesus. He gives hope that transcends this earthly life. And he has confirmed it through his resurrection from the dead.

The Gospel accounts reveal that though God has revealed himself in the face of Jesus Christ, people do not automatically come to know him or receive his everlasting life. For this, a belief response is needed on the part of every individual (Jn. 3:16-17, 19). However, one cannot make a belief-response by mere superficial feelings. Understanding or cognitive perception of the ultimate truth in Jesus makes it possible. This understanding or perception aided by the divine epistemic agent, the Holy Spirit, brings an individual into a saving relationship with the Father and the Son. Within this relationship with the Godhead (Father, Son and the Holy Spirit), a believer has access to further knowledge that stimulates discipleship and provides supports in sustaining one's saving relationship with Jesus. In this manner, the Gospels give clear evidence regarding the vital role of understanding or the cognitive function of the mind in coming to the knowledge of truth and subsequently making progress in discipleship. The theme of understanding in the Gospels presents us with the following challenges in relation to our discipleship:

1. Understanding is possible only in *being* with Jesus

2. Understanding is possible in *being* with fellow disciples

3. Understanding requires an obedient response to move further in discipleship

1. Understanding is possible only in *being* with Jesus
In the Gospels, we have seen that understanding about Lord Jesus Christ is not only possible through revelation from above, but in

continuing "with Jesus." This implies that growth in discipleship through increased understanding is not an outcome of solitary intellectual exercise. In the light of this, discipleship would mean absolute dependence upon God and a continual movement towards him, becoming better reflectors of his character and glory each day.

After Christ's ascension, the disciples were promised a comforter, who would continue to lead them in the teachings of Christ. Thus, Christian life can only be lived out by constantly abiding in the words of Jesus through the Holy Spirit. If Christian discipleship is like this, then it should cause us (the post-Easter disciples of Jesus Christ) to enhance rather than replace the practicing of solid biblical exegesis and developing our intellectual skills. In this way, we would be able to know the true wisdom needed to successfully navigate through life.

This knowledge informs us in the following ways:

- Disciples are called to ethical living
- Disciples are called to engage their minds in following Jesus
- Disciples are called to share the message meaningfully

Disciples are called to ethical living

The main purpose of theological studies cannot be seen purely in terms of acquiring head knowledge but a progressive quest for knowing Jesus and his instructions, with a desire to orient us according to the Jesus paradigm. Most of the uncertainties in the minds of disciples were the result of their failures to understand. These dark areas or misunderstandings shut down confidence and love, and we must never rest until they are cleanly dispersed from the mind. However, in doing this, we must remember that we are not counting our own cleverness or abilities, but stand in dependence on the Holy Spirit of truth who is constantly at work in the lives of the disciples of Jesus. When we move forward with such an attitude, the Holy Spirit facilitates our understanding (or cognitive perception), which leads to transformative knowledge. Since orthodoxy (right thinking) is inextricably linked to orthopraxis (right acting), the Spirit has a significant role in understanding the right morality. Therefore, a Spirit-informed epistemology must affect our lifestyle.

Disciples are called to engage their minds in following Jesus
In our times, churches are, by and large, marked by a strong emphasis on the emotions and outward conformity to church ordinances. Though traditions in themselves are not bad, traditions without serious thought dominate Christian culture nowadays, which is not a healthy sign. In connection with the modern Christianity, Henri Nouwen says:

> We simply go along with the many "musts" and "oughts" that have been handed on to us, and we live with them as if they were authentic translations of the Gospel of our Lord...Thus, the essence of Christianity is narrowed down to merely a consumer, or client, relationship to Jesus and his people.[1]

Discipleship is about continuing in learning. This was true for the disciples of Jesus. Though they became leaders, but they kept on learning. I believe that the expectation to blindly adhering to the traditions has caused many genuine men and women to discontinue going to church. Even though love stands out as the strongest motive to follow Jesus, it does not mean that understanding Jesus and his instructions could be bypassed. As any kind of irrational following does not produce much progress in discipleship, the followers are never able to fully understand the reasons for abiding in Jesus' words. The Church (gathering of disciples of Lord Jesus Christ) would not be able to make any significant progress as disciples of Jesus, unless they wrestle to understand and apply the Word of God using their intellectual abilities. This is why Jesus replied that the first and greatest command was to love God with all our heart, soul, strength and *mind* (Mk. 12:30). This includes loving God with our intellectual and cognitive faculties as well.

Discussing contemporary Christianity, Paul Washer, preacher and teacher, brings out a very significant point in his message based on Matthew 7:13-24. He says that one of the greatest heresies of the present evangelical Christianity is that just because a person has made a "sinner's prayers" in some meeting somewhere, he or she has received salvation and so to say a "visa to heaven." Washer shows from the Scriptures how biblical faith ought to be preceded and followed by repentance. Commenting on the life of disciple, he says that it should be characterised by a continuous turning away from sin and growing into holiness. This I believe can only happen when the disciples commit themselves to a life of studying the Scriptures in order to know more about God's desire for their lives. However, in our consumer-driven culture, we have enough antidotes for contemplation that prevent people from studying the Word of God. This holds a potential to influence us to the extent that we can be befuddled regarding the priorities of our lives.

A more subtle development of our generation has been in the area of our defining the "really important" things in life. For instance, the popular view dominant in almost all the cultures around the world maintains that philosophical thoughts about "deeper" questions, the "meaning of life", etc., are questions meant for philosophers and thinkers and that the more important things are one's career, standard of living and psychological needs. However, this doubtful stance regarding the "deeper questions" is not a result of thinking but an absence or relegation of thinking. Nevertheless, none of us is exempt from the pressures that such a cultural matrix exerts on everyone who is a part of it. Recently, I came across a song written by Kirk Franklin that presents exactly this human predicament. He requests God to keep him from mixing his priorities in life. The song is entitled Lose my Soul:[2]

Man I wanna tell you all something, Man.
Man I'm not gonna let these material thing's, get in my way,
I'm trying to get somewhere.
I'm trying to get somewhere,
That's real and pure and true and eternal.

Father God, I am clay in your hands,
Help me to stay that way through all life's demands,

'Cause they chip and they nag and they pull at me,
And every little thing I make up my mind to be,
Like I'm gonna be a daddy whose in the mix,
And I'm gonna be a husband who stays legit,
And I pray that I'm an artist who rises above,

The road that is wide and filled with self love,
Everything that I see draws me,
Though it's only in You that I can truly see that its a feast for the
eyes—a low blow to purpose.
And I'm a little kid at a three ring circus.

I don't want to gain the whole world, and lose my soul,
Don't wanna walk away, let me hear the people say.
I don't want to gain the whole world, and lose my soul,
Don't wanna walk away, let me hear the people say.

As disciples of Jesus our prayer ought to be that we may not allow the material things come in our way of our wholehearted commitment to being with, hearing and learning from and doing Jesus' commands. The call that Jesus placed upon the first disciples is the same he places upon us: to make the quest for understanding and participating in God's kingdom as the primary passion and not to get confused in our priorities and that we may continue to move forward by keeping the "main thing" as the main thing.

Similarly, the conclusion that Christian faith is not only compatible with thinking but consists of, requires and stimulates profoundest thinking also bears influence on the area of Christian experience. Some groups of disciples have a tendency to over emphasise the experiential or emotional side of salvation or the Christian faith to the extent that the cognitive dimension is almost relegated to the periphery. However, this position steals us away from the conviction that genuine discipleship involves our cognitive, volitional and affective facilities. If this be the case, it is quite reasonable to think that the Spirit, who facilitates knowledge, also enables the disciples to interpret and evaluate correctly their religious experiences on the basis of their newly received knowledge, (which as we have seen is possible by being in a filial relationship with Jesus). This knowledge therefore, should be used to evaluate (or "judge") doctrine, praxis and experience. This position I believe would prevent the disciples of Jesus from getting trapped into ideas and experiences that are not consistent with the dynamic and ongoing understanding of a disciple of Lord Jesus Christ.

Disciples are called to share the message meaningfully
In a country like India, where people have a religious disposition, it is believed that faith is a personal matter (of the heart) and so it should not be a matter of public discussion or rational debate. However, I am sure that Jesus or the Gospel writers would not buy into this kind of thinking. Yes, it is true that faith is a personal matter, but it has a message that can and needs to be clearly understood and meaningfully communicated (Mt. 28:18-20). This way of looking at Christian faith and evangelism challenges those who think they have a missionary zeal, but are caught up in the number game of "counting the heads." No wonder we hear about people going back to their previous lifestyles, turning their backs to Jesus. I believe Jesus is not interested in this type of number stunt. He is rather looking for those who follow and worship him in "spirit" as well as in *truth.*

At the same time, this also challenges the new disciples to examine their motives behind their following Christ. May be they have learnt the language used in the gathering of disciples, but they are there for entirely wrong reasons. These are the disciples who may also return from following Jesus when things do not move as they expect or when persecution and suffering hits them. This clearly highlights the importance of rational dimension in our evangelistic message, one that would produce nice and strong feelings and also generate deep-seated conviction. This is the reason why Apostle Peter exhorted, "Set apart Christ in your heart and always be ready to give a defense to everyone who asks you a reason for the hope that is in you, with meekness and fear" (1 Pet. 3:15). Since the disciples are sent into the world (Mt. 28:18-20; Jn. 17:15a; 20:21), it would require a serious engagement with the world. This would mean an up-to-date awareness and a critical appraisal of contemporary issues.

There is a general perception that biblical understanding is only meant for those in "full time" ministry. However, this understanding is meant for each and every person who calls himself or herself a disciple of Jesus Christ. Since faith is wrongly perceived as only a matter of the heart, the need to apply ones intellectual abilities to understand and share God's revelation becomes even more important.

2. Understanding is possible in *being* with fellow disciples
Right understanding that leads to growth in discipleship is not possible without a life connected with Jesus; it is also not possible without *being with other disciples*. This is perhaps what Jesus meant when he commanded the disciples to love one another and presented their mutual love as one of their distinguishing identification marks. Perhaps, loving one another was a challenge even during the first-century days, which led John the apostle to write again in his first epistle, "If someone says, 'I love God', and hates his brother, he is a liar; for he who does not love his brother whom he has seen, how can he love God whom he has not seen?" (1Jn. 4:20) Though the theological context may provide us with a mental and conceptual framework of God and His ongoing work, it is the relational context that unveils the personal orientation of discipleship. Perhaps, that is why Apostle Paul was led to write, "Knowledge puffs up, but love edifies (1 Cor. 8:1)." Ultimately the purpose of understanding is not to make big-headed disciples, who would find it difficult to balance their "big heads" on their shoulders and to handle people who have not acquired as much understanding as they have received. On the contrary, it is so that ultimately God's love would begin to dominate all our being to the extent that it would begin to overflow and touch the lives of our fellow brothers and sisters.

3. Understanding requires an obedient response to move further in discipleship

Though understanding plays a crucial role in the spiritual transformation of disciples of Jesus, the role of human "will" can nevertheless be minimised. We have seen that the problem with crowd and the religious leaders was not that they did not understand enough to make a faith response, but in their willful rejection of the words of Jesus. They stand as negative examples of discipleship. They tell us how not to respond to the instructions and commands of Jesus. Therefore, a radical form of commitment to obey the commands and to live according to them is needed. This would ensure the necessary application of the greatest commandment to love God with one's whole heart, soul, strength and mind.

There is a story about five frogs who were sitting on a log of wood beside a pond. They sat there discussing an important issue. This was their favorite spot, as it was near the pond where they lived and provided them with a comfortable place. It was a clear and sunny day and after some time, four of them decided to dive back into the pond. It would not require a scientist to tell the number of frogs left on the log of wood. Can you guess? One? Two? Four? Surprisingly, the answer is five. This is because four of them only *decided* to dive into the pond, but they did not *really* dive. This is how many of us behave as disciples of Jesus. Going to church and meticulously reading the Bible exposes us to biblical truths, but more often than not, we do not actually apply all that we learn. And so we are not able to make progress in our lives as disciples of Jesus.

It is possible that we may become too critical of the disciples' lack of understanding without recognising that they lived before the death and resurrection of Jesus. Consequently, we enter into an unhealthy criticism of the disciples. Had we been in their situation, perhaps we would have also acted and reacted in the same manner. Be that as it may, the important point is that we must recognise their role in shaping our lives. If the Lord expected complete devotion and obedience from his immediate disciples and felt frustrated when they failed to understand and acted in a self-centered manner, how much more would the Lord expect of us, who have been exposed to the complete revelation of the Word of God and sealed and blessed with the gift of the Holy Spirit.

Recommendations

The present study shows the importance of the theme of "incomprehension" or "misunderstanding" for all the four Evangelists. We have seen how understanding or the cognitive perception plays a crucial role in Christian discipleship and spiritual formation. However, we have also noted that this theme has not been adequately dealt with in theological circles. A question, let us say, about the relationship between understanding and human "will" and the extent to which human will is involved in making a belief-response need to be addressed. Similarly, academicians and believers must focus on how and to what extent the Spirit is involved in determining the ethics of the Gospel writers. The theme of understanding or cognitive perception and the idea of "truth" also need to be looked at from a philosophical perspective. Also, the issue of the extent to which the epistemologies of the Gospel writers inform, confirm or subvert contemporary epistemologies needs to be investigated. Thus, we see that the theme of incomprehension in the Gospels implores further academic research and the reader must endeavor to take the studies in this field to the next level.

End Notes

[1] Quoted in Willard, *The Divine Conspiracy: Rediscovering our Hidden Life in God* (London: Harper Collins, 1998), 304-04.

[2] *http://www.azlyrics.com/lyrics/tobymac/losemysoul.html* accessed on March 12, 2011.

Bibliography

Books

Balabanski, Vicky. *Eschatology in the Making*. SNTS Mon. Ser. 97. Oakleigh, Melbourne: Cambridge University Press, 1997.

Beck, Brian E. *Christian Character in the Gospel of Luke*. London: Epworth, 1989.

Bennema, Cornelis. *The Power of Saving Wisdom: An Investigation of Spirit and Wisdom in Relation to the Soteriology of the Fourth Gospel*. Tübingen: Mohr Siebeck, 2002.

Carter, Warren. *Matthew and the Margins: A Socio-Political and Religious Reading*. JSNT Suppl. Ser. 204. Sheffield: Sheffield Academic Press, 2000.

Collins, Raymond F. *These Things Have Been Written: Studies on the Fourth Gospel*. Louvain Theological and Pastoral Monograph, 2. Grand Rapids, Michigan: Eerdmans, 1990.

Cook, John G. *The Structure and Persuasive Power of Mark: A Linguistic Approach*. SBL Sem. Ser. Atlanta, Georgia: Scholars Press, 1995.

Conzelmann, Hans. *The Theology of St. Luke*. Trans. Geoffrey Buswell. New York: Harper & Row, 1953.

Culpepper, R. Alan. *Anatomy of the Forth Gospel: A Study in Literary Design*. Philadelphia: Fortress Press, 1983.

_____, *The Gospel and the Letters of John*. Interpreting Biblical Texts Series. Nashville: Abingdon, 1998.

Doohan, Leonard. *The Perennial Spirituality*. Santa Fee, New Mexico: Bears and Company Incorporation, 1982.

Esler, Philip Francis. *Community and Gospel in Luke-Acts: The Social And Political Motivations of Lucan Theology*. Cambridge: Cambridge University Press, 1987.

Forbes, Greg W. *The God of Old: The Role of the Lukan Parables in the Purpose of Luke's Gospel.* JSNT Suppl. Ser., 198. Sheffield: Sheffield Press, 2000.

France, R. T. *Matthew: Evangelist and Teacher.* Grand Rapids, Michigan: Academie Books (Zondervan), 1989.

Green, Joel B. *Theology of the Gospel of Luke.* NTT. Cambridge: Cambridge University Press, 1995.

Green, Michael. *The Message of Matthew.* BST. Leicester: IVP, 2000.

Heil, John Paul. *The Meal Scenes in Luke-Acts: An Audience-Oriented Approach.* Atlanta, Georgia: SBL. 1999.

Hargreaves, John. *A Guide to St. Mark's Gospel.* Cambridge: Cambridge University Press, 1965.

Kingsbury, Jack Dean. *Conflict in Luke: Jesus, Authorities, Disciples.* Minneapolis: Fortress Press, 1991.

_____, *Matthew as a Story.* 2d ed. Philadelphia: Fortress, 1988.

_____, *Matthew as a Story.* Philadelphia: Fortress Press, 1986.

Knight, Jonathan. *Luke's Gospel.* London: Routledge, 1998.

Kostenberger, Andreas J. *Encountering John: The Gospel in Historical, Literary and Theological Perspective.* Grand Rapids, Michigan: Baker, 1999.

_____, *The Mission of Jesus and the Disciples according to the Fourth Gospel.* Grand Rapids, Michigan: Baker, 1998.

Kysar, Robert. *John: The Maverick Gospel,* rev. ed. Louisville, Kentucky: Westminster, 1993.

Luz, Ulrich. *The Theology of the Gospel of Matthew.* NTT. Cambridge: Cambridge University Press, 1993.

Marshall, Christopher D. *Faith as a Theme in Mark's Narrative.* Cambridge: Cambridge University Press, 1989.

Marshall, I. Howard. *Luke: Historian and Theologian.* Flemington Markets, NSW: Paternoster, 1970.

McGrath, James F. *John's Apologetic Christology: Legitimation and Development in Johannine Christology.* SNTS Mon. Ser., 111. Cambridge: Cambridge University Press, 2001.

Moloney, Francis J. *Belief in the Word: John 1-4.* Minneapolis: Fortress Press, 1993.

_____, *Glory Not Dishonor: Reading John 13-21.* Minneapolis: Fortress Press, 1998.

Moody, Smith D. *The Theology of John*. NTT. Cambridge: Cambridge University Press, 1995.

Moreland, J. P. *Love Your God with All Your Mind: The Role of Reason in the Life of the Soul*. Colorado, Colorado Springs: Navpress, 1997.

Myers, Chad. *Binding the Strong Man: A Political Reading of Mark's Story of Jesus*. Maryknoll, NY: Orbis Books, 1997.

Nelson, Peter K. *Leadership and Discipleship: A Study of Luke 22:24-30*. SBL Diss. Ser. Georgia: Scholars Press, 1994.

Neyrey, Jerome H., ed. *The Social World of Luke-Acts: Models for Interpretation*. Peabody, Massachusetts: Hendrickson, 1991.

Overman, Andrew J. *Matthew's Gospel and Formative Judaism: The Social World of Matthean Community*. Minneapolis: Fortress, 1990.

Painter, John. *The Quest for the Messiah: The History, Literature and Theology of Johannine Community*. Edinburgh: T&T Clark, 1991.

Palmer, Earl F. *The Intimate Gospel*. Waco, Texas: Word, 1978.

Peterson Dwight N. *The Origins of Mark: The Markan Community in Current Debate*. Netherlands, Leiden: Brill, 2000.

Peterson, Robert A. *Getting to Know John's Gospel: A Fresh Look at Its Main Ideas*. Philipsburg, New Jersey: Presbyterian and Reformed Publishing Company, 1989.

Pilgrim, Walter E. *Good News to the Poor: Wealth and Poverty in Luke-Acts*. Minneapolis, Minnesota: Augsburg Publication House, 1981.

Rhoads, David, Joanna Dewey, and Donald Michie. *Mark as a Story: An Introduction to the Narrative of a Gospel*, 2nd ed. Minneapolis: Fortress Press, 1999.

Riches, John K. *Conflicting Mythologies: Identity Formation in the Gospel of Mark and Matthew*. SNTW. Edinburgh: T&T Clark, 2000.

Riches, John, William R. Telford, and Christopher M. Tuckett, eds. *The Synoptic Gospels*. With an Introduction by Scot McKnight. Sheffield: Sheffield Press, 2001.

Segovia, Fernando F, ed. *What is John?* Literary And Social Readings of the Fourth Gospel, vol. II. Atlanta, Georgia: Scholars Press, 1998.

Shiner, Whitney P. *Follow Me! Disciples in Mark*. SBL Diss. Ser., 145. Atlanta, Georgia: Scholars Press, 1995.

Sim, David C. *The Gospel of Matthew and Christian Judaism: The History and Social Setting of the Matthean Community*. Edinburgh: T&T Clark, 1988.

_____, *Apocalyptic Eschatology in the Gospel of Matthew.* SNTS Mon. Ser., 88. Cambridge: Cambridge University Press, 1996.

Smalley, Stephen S. *John, Evangelist and Interpreter,* 2d ed. Downers Grove, Illinois: IVP, 1998.

Smith, D. Moody. *The Theology of the Gospel of John.* NTT. Cambridge: Cambridge University Press, 1995.

Stein, Robert H. *The Synoptic Problem: An Introduction.* Nottingham: IVP, 1988.

Telford, W. R. *The Theology of the Gospel of Mark.* NTT. Cambridge: Cambridge Press, 1999.

Tuckett, Christopher M. *Luke.* NT Guides. Sheffield: Sheffield Press, 1996.

Watts, Ricci E. *Isaiah's New Exodus in Mark.* Grand Rapids, Michigan: Eerdmans, 1997.

Wilkins, Michael J. *Discipleship in the Ancient World and Matthew's Gospel,* 2nd ed. Grand Rapids, Michigan: Baker Book House, 1995.

_____, *Following the Master: Discipleship in the Steps of Jesus.* Grand Rapids, Michigan: Zondervan, 1992.

Willard, Dallas. *The Divine Conspiracy: Rediscovering Our Hidden Life in God.* London: Harper Collins, 1998.

Commentaries

Anderson, Hugh. *The Gospel of Mark.* The New Century Bible Commentary. Grand Rapids, Michigan: Eerdmans, 1981.

Beasley-Murray George R. *John 1-16.* WBC, vol. 36. Waco, Texas: Word Books, 1987.

Bock, D. L. *Luke.* The IVP New Testament Commentary Series. Leicester: IVP, 1994.

Brook, Wes Howard. *Becoming Children of God: John's Gospel and Radical Discipleship.* New York: Orbis, 1994.

Brown, Raymond F. *The Gospel According to John I – XII.* ABC. New York: Doubleday, 1966.

Evans, Craig A. *Mark 8:1-16:20.* WBC, vol. 34B, Dallas, Texas: Word Publishing, 1989.

Gould, Ezra P. *Mark.* International Critical Bible Commentary. Edinburgh: T&T Clark, 1982.

Hendriksen, William. *Mark.* New Testament Commentary. Edinburgh: The Banner of Truth Trust, 1975.

Keck, Leander E, ed. *The New Interpreter's Bible.* Vol. VIII. Nashville, Abingdon Press, 1995.

Keener, Craig S. *Matthew.* The IVP New Testament Commentary Series. Leicester, England: IVP, 1997.

Lane, William. *Gospel of Mark.* The New Commentary of the New Testament. London: Morgan Marshall & Scott Company, 1974.

Marcus, Joel. *Mark 1-8.* ABC. New York: Doubleday, 2000.

Marshall, I. Howard. *The Gospel of Luke. A Commentary on the Greek Text.* NIGTC. Grand Rapids, Michigan: Eerdmans, 1978.

Nolland, John. *Luke 1-9:20.* WBC, vol. 35A. Waco, Texas: Word Books, 1983.

―――――――, *Luke 9:21-18:34.* WBC, vol. 35B. Waco, Texas: Word Books, 1993.

Ridderbos, Herman. *The Gospel of John: A Theological Commentary.* Grand Rapids, Michigan: Eerdmans, 1987.

Witherington III, Ben. *John's Wisdom: A Commentary on the Fourth Gospel.* Louisville, Kentucky: Westminster John Knox Press, 1995.

―――――――, *The Rhetoric of Mark: A Socio Rhetorical Commentary.* Grand Rapids, Michigan: Eerdmans, 2001.

Articles

Allison, D. C. "Apocalypse." In *DJG*, eds. Joel B. Green and Scot McKnight, 17-20. Leicester: IVP, 1992.

Barton, Stephen. "Gospel Wisdom." In *Where Shall Wisdom be Found*, ed. Stephen Barton, 93-110. Edinburgh: T&T Clark, 1999.

Bandstra, B and S. S. Stuart. "Mind." In *The International Standard Bible Encyclopedia*, ed. Geoffrey W. Bromiley, vol. III, 362-63. Grand Rapids, MI: Eerdmans, 1979.

Bennema Cornelis, 'Christ, the Spirit and the Knowledge of God: A Study in Johannine Epistemology' in M. Healy and R. Parry (eds.), *The Bible and Epistemology: Biblical Soundings on the Knowledge of God* (Milton Keynes: Paternoster, 2007) 107-133.

Behm. καρδια. In *TDNT*, ed. Gerhard Kittel, vol. III, 605-14. Grand Rapids, Michigan: Eerdmans, 1965.

―――――――, noew. In *TDNT*, ed. Gerhard Kittel, vol. IV, 948-980. Grand Rapids, Michigan: Eerdmans, 1965.

Bock, D. L. "Luke, Gospel of." In *DJG*, eds. Joel B. Green and Scott McKnight, 495- 510. Downers Grove, Ill.: IVP, 1992.

118 THE ROLE OF THE MIND IN DISCIPLESHIP

Dunn, James D. G. "Where Shall Wisdom be Found." In *Where Shall Wisdom be Found*, ed. Stephen C. Barton, 74-93. Edinburgh: T&T Clark, 1999.

Geddert, Timothy J. "Apocalyptic Teaching." In *DJG*, eds. Joel B. Green and Scot McKnight, 20-27. Leicester: IVP, 1992.

Green, Joel B. "Death of Jesus." In *DJG*, eds. Joel B. Green and Scot McKnight, 146-63. Leicester, England: IVP, 1992.

Horsley, Richard. "Wisdom and Apocalypticism in Mark." In *In Search of Wisdom: Essays in Memory of John G. Gammie*, eds. Leo G. Perdue, et al., 223-244. Louisville, Kentucky: Westminster, 1993.

Luz, Ulrich. "The Disciples in the Gospel according to Matthew." In *The Interpretation of Matthew*, ed. Graham Stanton, 115-148. Edinburgh: T&T Clark, 1995.

Rowland, Christopher. "Sweet Science Reigns: Divine and Human Wisdom in Apocalyptic Tradition." In *Where Shall Wisdom be Found*, ed. Stephen C. Barton, 61-73. Edinburgh: T&T Clark, 1999.

Schweizer, Eduard. "Matthew's Church." In *The Interpretation of Matthew*, ed. Graham Stanton, 149-177. Edinburgh: T&T Clark, 1995.

Scott, Bernard Brandon. "The Gospel of Matthew: A Sapiential Performance of an Apocalyptic Discourse." In *In Search of Wisdom: Essays in Memory of John G. Gammie*, eds. Leo G. Perdue et al., 245-262. Louisville, Kentucky: Westminster, 1993.

The Little Oxford English Dictionary. Eighth Edition. ed. Angus Stevenson with Julia Elliot and Richard Jones. Oxford: Oxford University Press, 2002.

Thompson, M. M. "John, Gospel of." In *DJG*, eds. Joel B Green and Scot McKnight, 368-383. Leicester, England: IVP, 1992.

Tuckett, C.M. "Synoptic Problem." In *ABD*, ed. David Noel Freedman, vol. 6, 263-270. New York: Doubleday, 1992.

Wilkins, M J. "Discipleship." In *DJG*, eds. Joel B. Green and Scot McKnight, 182-189. Leicester: IVP, 1992.

Journal Articles

Gundry, Robert H. "On True and False Disciples in Matthew 8.18-22." *JNTS* 40 (1994): 433-441.

Kingsbury, Jack Dean. "The Rhetoric of Comprehension in the Gospel of Matthew." *NTS* 41 (1995): 358-377.

Marcus, Joel. "Mark 4:10-12 and Marcan Epistemology." *JBL* 103, no 4 (1984): 557-574.

Tyson, Joseph B. "The Blindness of the Disciples in Mark". *JBL* 80, no 2 (Sept. 1961): 261-268.

CD-Rom

Beasley-Murray, George R. "Enigma of the Gospel." In *WBC*, ed. Bruce M. Metzger, vol. 36. CD ROM. (accessed on November 05, 2004).

Websites

Best, Ernest. "Why is Mark so hard on the Disciples?" *http://users.ox.ac.uk/~sben0056/essays/markandthedisciples.htm* accessed on January 25, 2011

Clemons, Cheryl. "Loving God With the Mind - Christian Discipleship and the Role of the Intellect: Insight from John Henry Newman" *www.umass.edu/catholic/campus/conf/LovingGodWiththeMind.doc;* (Accessed on June 07, 2004).

Israel, Martin. "Doubt", *www.Martinisrael.u-net/doubt/chapter13.html;* (Accessed on August 03, 2004).

Smith, Aarry. "Jesus as Teacher in the Synoptic Gospels." *http://www.abu.nb.ca/Courses/NTIntro/LifeJ/TeacherJesus.htm;* (Accessed on July 15, 2004).

Stanford Encyclopedia of Philosophy, *http://plato.stanford.edu/entries/kant-religion/* accessed on January 25, 2011

http://www.annabelle.net/topics/author.php?firstname=Lord&lastname= Tennyson. (Accessed on June 08, 2004)

9 7 8 8 1 8 4 6 5 1 4 2 3